Jewish Fairy Tale Feasts

A Literary Cookbook

First paperback edition published in 2020 by **Crocodile Books**
An imprint of Interlink Publishing Group, Inc.
46 Crosby Street, Northampton, Massachusetts 01060
www.interlinkbooks.com

LIBRARY OF CONGRESS CATALOGING-IN-PUBLICATION DATA

Yolen, Jane, author.
Jewish fairy tale feasts / stories retold by Jane Yolen; recipes by Heidi E.Y. Stemple;
illustrations by Sima Elizabeth Shefrin. -- First American edition.   pages cm
Includes bibliographical references and index.
ISBN 978-1-56656-909-5 (hardcover) 978-1-56656-040-5 (paperback)
1. Jewish cooking--Juvenile literature. 2. Fairy tales. I. Stemple, Heidi E. Y., author. II.
Shefrin, Sima Elizabeth, 1949- illustrator. III. Title.
TX724.Y65 2012   641.5'676--dc23   2012016174

Book design by Elisa Gutiérrez

10 9 8 7 6 5 4 3 2 1

Printed and bound in China.

Jewish Fairy Tale Feasts

A Literary Cookbook

Tales retold by **Jane Yolen**   Recipes by **Heidi E.Y. Stemple**

Illustrations by **Sima Elizabeth Shefrin**

Crocodile Books, USA

An imprint of Interlink Publishing Group, Inc.

www.interlinkbooks.com

For the great eaters in both the Yolen and Stemple families. —JY

• •

For Jason Messier, who cooks for my daughter.
With love, your Jewish mother (in law). —HEYS

• •

For Bob. —SES

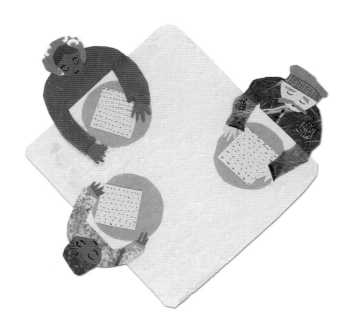

CONTENTS

8   Stories and Stovetops Jewish-Style: An Introduction

10   A Note from the Storyteller

11   A Note from the Cook

❖ BRUNCH ❖

14   The Latke Miracle
20   Latkes

24   The Three Skillful Brothers
30   Applesauce

34   Counting Eggs
40   Shakshuka

44   The Demon Who Lived in a Tree
52   Blintzes

58   And the Matzo Was Still Warm
66   Matzo Brei

70   The Loaves in the Ark
76   Challah

82   The Wheat Came in at the Door
86   Bagels

❖ SOUP ❖

92   A Little Bit of Soup
98   Chicken Soup

102   The Flour Barrel and the Water Jug
106   Matzo Balls

❖ MAIN COURSES ❖

112 Rifka and the Magic Pitcher
120 Salad

124 The Pomergranate Seed
128 Pomergranate Couscous

132 How to Know a Noodle
136 Noodle Kugel

140 The Hair in the Milk
146 Matzo Lasagna

150 Three Clever Things
158 Tzimmes Chicken

❖ DESSERT ❖

164 The Pastry That Was Eternally Dirty
168 Rugalach

172 The Congregation That Loved Jam
176 Hamantaschen

180 Two Jars of Honey
188 Honey Cake

192 The Little Cap-Wearers and the Cow
196 Mini Cheesecakes

Stories and Stovetops Jewish-Style: An Introduction

There is a popular Jewish folktale about a king who visits the house of a poor Jewish family on a Sabbath eve and is invited to share their humble meal. Every Sabbath eve—Friday night—there is a ritual meal with prayers over the food.

So the king comes in, sees the table spread with a gleaming white tablecloth and alight with candles. He sits down amid the gathered family. The food is brought out: chicken soup, challah, kugel, tzimmes. None of these are dishes the king has ever tasted.

The Hebrew prayers are said. Then the Sabbath Queen—the spirit who rules over the Sabbath—is called. Songs are sung. Everyone at the table is joyous because that is how the Sabbath is greeted in a Jewish home.

And the king? He thinks it is the greatest meal he has ever had. He sends his cook the next week to learn the recipes from the woman of the house.

But in his palace the food is tasteless.

Thinking the Jew has played a trick on him, the king returns with his soldiers, ready to arrest the poor man, until the man and his wife explain: ingredients and cooking alone do not make a Sabbath meal. It is the prayers, candles, and the joy of looking for-ward to the Sabbath day that make everything taste so wonderful.

And so the king goes home, greater in understanding of the Jewish people in his kingdom.

. . . .

Now, not everyone Jewish cooks Jewish food. But most of the people who cook it have their own recipes, handed down generation to generation. The recipes differ from family to family because Jews have lived in every country of the world. And of course, every Jewish holiday has its special dishes.

Many religious and/or traditional Jews keep to the kosher (*kashrut*) laws, which outline just what foods can and cannot be eaten: No pork, no shellfish, no mixing meat and milk foods in the same meal, etc. Some of the kosher laws may seem odd to outsiders, but for the kosher Jewish cooks and eaters, they are important both as ritual and as metaphor for the way to live a righteous life. Many of these laws began as a way to distinguish Jews from non-Jews, or to help Jews maintain a religious discipline, or to promote hygiene at a time when little was known about germs or the humane care of animals. As one rabbi has put it, kosher laws elevate eating to "a level of holiness."

The stories, too, use food both as a link between human and the holy. Many of them come from times of near-starvation, or are about traditional trickster characters like Hershel Ostropolier, or traditional holy characters such as the prophet Elijah, who singles out good people with his magical gifts when they share what little food they have with a stranger. Other stories are traveling tales that can be found in many cultures, for the Jews have spent countless years as guests or servants, workers or slaves, teachers or advisors within larger nations.

But even more important is the tie between stories and recipes. Think about it: both are constantly changing, suiting the needs of the maker and the consumer. A storyteller never tells the same story in exactly the same way because every audience needs a slightly different tale, depending upon the season, the time of day, the restlessness of the youngest listener, or even what has happened recently in the news. And of course every cook knows how recipes change, according to weather conditions, altitude, the number of grains in a level teaspoon, the ingredients in the cupboard or refrigerator, the tastes or allergies of the dinner guests—even the cook's own feelings about the look of the batter or the smell of the soup.

So be playful with both these stories and recipes. First make/tell them exactly as they are here, and then begin to experiment. Recipes and stories are made more beautiful, more filling, more memorable by what *you* put in them.

. . . .

It was once said by a wit that all Jewish history could be summed up this way: "They tried to kill us. We won. Let's eat." And while obviously not strictly true, there are many stories about food, eating, and wars both in the Torah—the Jewish Bible—and in the folklore of the Jewish people.

So—let's eat!

Jane Yolen and Heidi E.Y. Stemple

A Note from the Storyteller

All the stories in this book are retold by me, but they come out of the vast storehouse of Jewish tales that are thousands of years old. When a storyteller retells a folktale, she seeks as many versions as possible, understands the story structure, and only then tells it in her own words.

What have I added to the stories as I retold them? Names, places, dialogue, descriptions, rhymes. Sometimes I even stick in pieces of other stories. I look for new ways to say old things. And as I work, I always read the story aloud. The eye and the ear are different listeners.

I also wrote the notes at the end of each tale and each recipe throughout this book. (And then Heidi rewrote them. Then I rewrote her rewriting until we were both satisfied with the end result.) These notes tell you where each story and recipe came from or what other stories or recipes they relate to, and how and where each story and recipe has traveled on its journey to this book. The notes also give you historical and cultural information.

When I talk about a "tale type," I am referring to the Aarne-Thompson Index, also known as "The Types of the Folktale." This is the earliest and most import system of grouping stories (mostly European tales) by reference numbers according to their themes, and was first developed in 1910 by Finnish folklorist Antti Aarne and later enlarged by American folklorist Stith Thompson in 1928. It was updated again in 1961, which is when I first came upon it. The system helps folktale researchers see which stories share common themes or building-block incidents. So open your eyes, your ears, your heart—and enjoy the tales.

A Note from the Cook

I am not a chef. I am a mom who loves cooking with her kids. The recipes in this book have been collected, written, and tested by me. They all have Jewish tradition in them, whether they are recipes deeply rooted in history, or modern interpretations.

When I was growing up, my mom preferred telling stories to cooking. So while plenty of stories were passed down, there were very few recipes, Jewish or otherwise. This means that for this book, I had to start from scratch.

Like stories, recipes are ever-evolving—changed by every hand that touches them. In my house, I cook according to the likes and dislikes of my daughters, Maddison and Glendon. But that does not mean these recipes will suit every eater's tastes. When you cook, make the recipes your own. Change ingredients according to how you like to eat. Use the tools you have in your kitchen, which may not always be the same as mine. In fact, that is how many traditional Jewish foods came to be. Recipes were brought in or borrowed from neighboring cultures and changed according to the ingredients, the tools at hand, and the specific rules of the faith.

This is not a kid's cookbook. It is a cookbook for kids. You're not going to find recipes for peanut butter and jelly sandwiches. You will find recipes for real meals. The cooking will involve knives and stoves. Make sure you have adult supervision. Even if you don't think you are ready to cook a whole meal, there are jobs for young chefs of all ages and abilities.

Remember safe kitchen rules. Be careful. Pull back your hair if it is long. Wash your hands before, after, and during the food preparation. And have fun. Cooking should not only be about eating. The food tastes so much better when you enjoy the whole process. So grab a mixing bowl and a spatula... and let's cook!

Heidi ey Spl

❖ BRUNCH ❖

The Latke Miracle
Latkes

The Three Skillful Brothers
Applesauce

Counting Eggs
Shakshuka

The Demon Who Lived in a Tree
Blintzes

And the Matzo Was Still Warm
Matzo Brei

The Loaves in the Ark
Challah

The Wheat Came in at the Door
Bagels

The Latke Miracle

"Eating latkes makes you a well-rounded person."
—Jewish saying

Once, in the old country, there was a widow with seven children. Seven! You can imagine how hard it was to feed them all. She worked hard, scrimping and saving and watering things down.

As Hanukkah approached, the youngest child—a girl named Chana—looked up at her mother with pleading eyes. "Mama," she said, "we have not had latkes, pancakes, all year long. Surely we will have them for Hanukkah."

"Yes, latkes!" the rest of the children chimed in. "With applesauce on top! Syrup! Jam!" Their list of toppings was endless.

Oh, how the widow's heart ached. More than anything she wanted to give them the Hanukkah meal they asked for. But there was no money in the house. Not a single penny. Nevertheless, she told them, "Wait here in the house, sweep the floor, dust, and make the place ready for the holiday. I will go to the river to rinse out the pots and buy flour from the miller for the latkes."

So off she went, appalled that she had told an untruth, hoping as ever for a miracle. She rinsed the pots in the river, and then— lost in her own thoughts—she stood, turned, and almost bumped into an old man who was standing next to her. If she'd done so, she'd have knocked him over, for he was quite thin, with an old hat upon his head.

"*Shalom*, peace to you," the old man said. "I am a stranger here, madam. I want to celebrate the holiday with a family but have none. Could you take me in?"

The widow never hesitated, for isn't it a *mitzvah*, a good deed, to take in a stranger on a holiday eve? And weren't her children, even now, making the house shine? "It would be our honor, old sir," she told him. "Our home is even now being readied for a guest."

No sooner had she given him this invitation than the old man disappeared. Down the road? Up the road? She couldn't see him. Had she insulted him? But even as she worried, she was relieved, because there was little enough for the children, much less a guest.

When she got home, all seven of her children were standing in the doorway, jumping up and down with joy.

"Mama, Mama," cried little Chana, "guess what!"

The widow smiled. Even when they had nothing, her children managed to make her smile. "I guess you are happy that Hanukkah is almost here …"

"No, Mama," said Daniel, the oldest, almost a man, "we are happy because an old gentleman came by and gave us Hanukkah money." He held out his hand. There were seven copper coins, one for each child. And a silver coin for the widow.

Shifre, the oldest girl, held out a large clay jug. "And he gave us this jug of oil for the Hanukkah lights."

Then all the children cried out together, "And a bag of flour, too."

"A bag of flour?" The widow clapped her hands. "Now I will make us all latkes. Children, see—it is a Hanukkah miracle."

The oil lasted eight days, just as it had in the temple in Jerusalem all those many years ago. The mixture for the latkes

made so many pancakes that the children grew full and happy.
And the coins—well, somehow they never ran out.

"Mama," little Chana whispered, "was the old man the prophet
Elijah?"

The widow gave her daughter a hug. "Who else," she said. "And he is welcome back any time he chooses to visit again."

But one miracle per family was all that Elijah ever handed out. And that one miracle was all that the widow and her seven children really needed.

I FOUND TWO VERY DIFFERENT TELLINGS OF THIS STORY, *one in Barbara Rush's* The Book of Jewish Women's Tales, *the other in Barbara Diamond Goldin's collection* Journeys with Elijah.

Elijah the prophet, the classic Jewish miracle maker, has the ability to travel through time. In the stories, he often does small miracles for people who invite him willingly into their homes.

Hanukkah (or Chanukah) is a winter holiday also known as the Festival of Lights. It celebrates the time the Maccabees rebelled against King Antiochus, who was trying to force the Jews to worship the way he did. Antiochus' troops had destroyed a major temple, and when the Maccabees retook it, they had to purify it. There was only enough sacred oil left to light one small lamp, but miraculously it burned for eight days. This is why the Hanukkah candelabra—the menorah—*has places for eight candles and a ninth called the* shamash, *or helper candle. And this is also why Hanukkah is celebrated for eight days.*

Hanukkah gelt *is Hanukkah money. In fact this is the only Jewish holiday whose celebration centers around the gift of money. These days, the* gelt *is most often candy money—chocolate wrapped in gold to look like coins. Some scholars think this goes back to the time of the Maccabees, who, after winning their war, minted the new nation's coins.*

Latkes (Potato Pancakes)

Latkes may be traditionally served for Hanukkah, but we like them all year long. I like mine with sour cream, but my daughters top them with homemade applesauce.

MAKES 12 SERVINGS

INGREDIENTS

4   medium potatoes (when grated, approximately 4 cups)

1   small onion (when grated, approximately ⅓ cup)

2   tbsp all-purpose flour

2   eggs

½   tsp salt

oil (for frying: vegetable, canola, or corn, but most oils will work)

Toppings:

sour cream

applesauce (see recipe, page 30)

EQUIPMENT

- vegetable peeler
- grater, or food processor with grater disc knife
- colander, clean cheesecloth, or towel (for draining the potatoes)
- large bowl
- fork
- large frying pan
- spatula and/or tongs
- plate with paper towels
- cutting board
- knife
- measuring spoon

1. Peel, wash, and grate the potatoes, and put them in a colander in the sink.

2. Crack the eggs into the bottom of a large bowl and beat with a fork.

3. Choose how you want to drain the potatoes: With clean hands, squeeze handfuls of the potatoes over the colander to drain off some of the water in them. Or, drain the liquid by wrapping the potatoes in cheesecloth or a clean towel. Holding the top of the cloth, twist the potato ball until it's tight and water is being squeezed out of it. Work in batches if needed. Once you're done, put the drained potatoes into the bowl with the eggs.

4. Cut off the ends of the onion and remove the first layer of skin. Grate the onion and add to the potatoes.

5. Add the flour and salt, and mix it all together. I like to do this with my hands.

6. Put about a ¼ inch of oil in the large frying pan and heat on medium–high.

7. When the oil is hot (you can test it by dropping in one potato shred; if it is hot, the potato will dance and sizzle in the oil), scoop a handful of the potato mixture and mold it into a pancake, then gently, so as not to splash hot oil, slide one potato pancake, then another, into the pan. Leave room between the pancakes to turn them.

8. When the underside has golden highlights, turn the pancake carefully with a spatula or tongs.

9. When each latke is finished cooking, set it on a plate lined with a paper towel to drain.

10. Top with sour cream or applesauce... or both.

LATKES COULD NOT HAVE BEEN MADE *of potatoes in old times because potatoes are a New World food, not brought to Europe until the eighteenth century. Perhaps, instead, latkes in olden times were made of grated cheese and egg.*

Potato pancakes are popular in many cuisines in Eastern Europe, like Czech, Ukrainian, German, Polish, and Russian. They are also the national dish of Belarus.

Potato pancakes may be eaten with a large variety of toppings: sour cream and applesauce are the most popular for Hanukkah latkes. But cinnamon, sugar, green onions, and a variety of jams and syrups are also used.

Hanukkah is the traditional time for Jews to have latkes, and the oil used to cook them reminds us of the miracle of the oil lamps.

Some cooks believe that "the starchier the potato, the crisper the latke."

The Three Skillful Brothers

"The reddest apple may have a worm."
—Jewish saying

Once long ago in the Great Middle East, there were three Jewish boys who were both good brothers and good friends. They lived happily with their father, for their mother was long in her grave.

But one day, Death, that old leveler, took their father, too, and the young men were saddened to discover that there was no money for their inheritance. Indeed, their family home had to be sold to pay their father's debts.

Still, they did not blame him, for he had been a good father. So they decided that each one would go in a different direction, and they promised to meet up again in five years to see how things had turned out.

The eldest brother apprenticed to a Persian rug maker who taught him so well that, by the end of his fifth year, the young man made a carpet that could fly him halfway around the world in the blink of an eye. On this very carpet he rode home in time to meet his brothers.

The middle brother apprenticed to an Egyptian mirror and lens maker. By the end of the fifth year, the young man was so skilled he made a mirror that could see halfway around the world. Then he rode home on a donkey, the mirror wrapped carefully in linen.

The youngest brother apprenticed to a local gardener. He learned the magic of seed and earth, sun, and rain. By the end of the fifth year, he had grafted two golden apple trees together and the result was a tree that grew apples so pure they could cure any sickness. But the tree only put forth one apple every generation. Storing this apple in the front of his shirt, the youngest brother trudged home just in time to meet his brothers.

What a happy reunion! Since the house was no longer theirs, they sat under a palm tree and ate, drank, reminisced. At last each brought out his treasure.

"Surely my flying carpet is the best," said the eldest brother.

"Surely my magic mirror is the best," said the middle brother.

The youngest smiled. "My apple can cure even those near death."

"Let us test them," proposed the older two together, and the youngest agreed.

The middle brother set his mirror against the palm tree and said,

Mirror, mirror, tell me true,
Is there something we must do?

The mirror grew misty, then cleared. As if looking through a window and not a mirror, the brothers could see a princess lying ill in bed. She was beautiful, with hair black as night, skin white as sea foam. Her father, the king, sat weeping by her bed, while viziers and advisors and rabbis ran around helplessly.

"Can we save her?" the middle brother asked.

"Only if we get there in time," said the eldest. "Quick—climb on my rug."

All three climbed aboard, along with the magic mirror, the golden apple, and the donkey, which took up rather more than its share of the rug. The young men sat cross-legged, and the donkey lay down beside them.

Then, showing the mirror's picture to the rug, the eldest brother said,

> *Rug, rush through the skies,*
> *Bring us to the girl who dies.*

The wind rushed under the rug, pushing and tugging. Slowly the rug rose into the air, and at once they were whisked through the sky so fast they had to hold on to their skullcaps or lose them.

As soon as they had begun, they were at their destination. The carpet settled down on a piece of grass within sight of the palace. The three brothers got off the carpet, rolled it up, placed it on the donkey, and off they went to save the dying princess.

When the guards at the gate questioned the brothers, they replied, "We are here to heal the princess."

So they were led into the throne room.

"If you cannot cure my daughter," the king said, "you will be hanged. But if one of you saves her, you will be married to her as soon as she can dance at her wedding, and will be king after me. Your brothers will serve as your ministers."

The eldest said, "Be ready to be amazed, sire."

So they were led into the princess' room, where she lay as still as death, her dark hair in two long braids.

The brothers sent everyone out of the room, and the eldest

said, "It is up to you now, youngest brother. If you cannot do what you have promised, we are all dead men."

The youngest looked not at his brothers but at the princess, who, even ill, was the most beautiful woman he'd ever seen. "If I cannot cure her," he said, "life would not be worth living anyway."

He took the apple from his shirt, plump and golden as the day he'd plucked it from the tree. He cut the apple into four pieces, and put the first slice to the princess' lips.

She stirred, licked the apple, opened her mouth, and he popped the apple in.

The princess sat up and began chewing the apple. "More!" she said.

At the sound of his daughter's voice, the king ran into the room. "She speaks!" he cried. "I haven't heard that beautiful sound in months."

The youngest brother gave the princess the second slice of apple, and then the third. By the fourth, she was out of bed and twirling around the room, singing.

The king clapped his hands. "She will marry one of you—but which one?"

"We wouldn't have gotten here in time without my flying rug," said the eldest brother.

"We would not even have known of the princess without my magic mirror," said the middle brother.

"She would have died anyway without my apple," said the youngest.

But all three together said, "We cannot make the decision."

The king called the rabbis together, and they wrestled with the problem for hours.

At last, the princess spoke up. "I can solve this puzzle," she said. Turning to the oldest brother, she said, "I honor you for the help you have given. Is your rug still intact?"

He bowed. "It is, princess. And ready to fly anywhere you wish."

"And your magic mirror," she said to the middle brother, "is it whole?"

He bowed, "It is, princess. And ready for you to gaze as you will."

Then she turned to the youngest, whose face was shining with love for her. "And the apple?"

"I gave it all to you, princess," he said.

"Then I give all of me to you," she said. "My sisters shall marry your brothers, who will make fine ministers."

And so it was.

In their long and happy marriage, the princess and the youngest brother shared a secret no one else knew: he'd kept the apple seeds. They planted those seeds together and tended them carefully so that in the next generation there would be another golden apple.

THIS STORY IS POPULAR AROUND THE WORLD, *but I found the Jewish version in Dov Noy's* Folktales of Israel. *That version was quite modern, so I reworked it, returning it to its Middle Eastern roots.*

The story belongs to Tale Type 653A, "The Skillful Brothers."

In a number of other versions, the princess solves the problem alone. However, this is the only version that reminds us that although the youngest brother gave away the apple, he kept the seeds.

Applesauce

The only recipe that was handed down from my great-grand-mother to my mother and then to me is for applesauce. If you have never had it made fresh, you won't believe how amazing it is when it is still warm from cooking.

MAKES 2 CUPS

INGREDIENTS

6   large apples (Macintosh or Granny Smith recommended)

¼   cup water

1   cinnamon stick or ¼ tsp ground cinnamon

    sugar (optional), 1 tbsp to ½ cup, depending on how sweet you like your applesauce

EQUIPMENT

- cutting board
- knife, apple corer, or apple cutter
- measuring cup
- measuring spoon
- large pot with lid
- large spoon
- wire colander or food mill
- large bowl

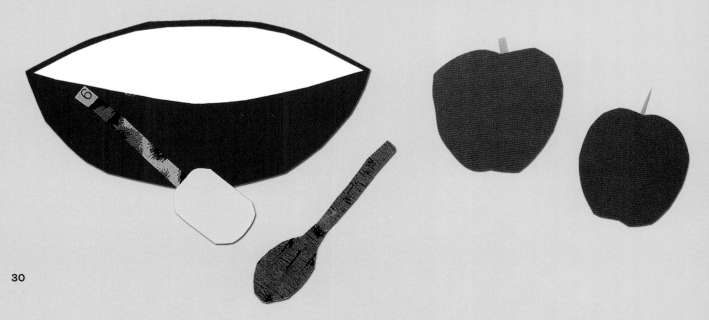

1. Rinse apples.

2. Core and cut apples into medium-sized chunks (leaving the skins on) with a knife, a knife and corer, or an apple cutter.

3. Put apples in a large pot and add the water and cinnamon, as well as sugar if you want sweet applesauce.

4. Heat on high until it reaches a boil, then turn the heat down to low-medium, cover the pot, and cook, stirring occasionally, for 15 to 20 minutes, or until all the apples are mushy and the skins are peeling off. Different types of apples take their own time to get to this point, so if they need another 5 minutes, let them have it.

5. Place a colander or food mill in a large bowl, and pour or scoop the apples into it.

6. Mash the apples:

—For colander: use a wooden spoon or spatula to press the apples through the colander.

—For food mill: grind the apples by turning the handle.

7. The applesauce will be caught in the bowl. Don't forget to scrape the underside of the colander or food mill.

8. Add more sugar if you want the applesauce sweeter.

VARIATIONS: *Use different types of apples. We like Macintosh the best and Granny Smith second. The type of apple you use changes the taste as well as the color of the applesauce. Try using cranberry juice, fresh-squeezed orange juice, or white wine instead of water.*

THE USUAL TRANSLATION INTO ENGLISH *for the fruit that Eve took from the tree in Eden is apple, though apples didn't grow in the Middle East. A better translation would be simply fruit, or specifically, a pomegranate, fig, or date.*

Apples and honey together are a Rosh Hashanah favorite, often apple slices dipped in honey. The roundness of the apple is a metaphor for the year; the honey symbolizes the sweetness to come. In fact, during Rosh Hashanah, nothing bitter or sour is eaten.

Apples are also favored on other holidays. Applesauce is spread on latkes at Hanukkah, and on Tu Bishvat—the "New Year of the Trees"—all kinds of tree fruits are eaten, but especially apples.

In northern Germany, Russia, Poland, and the Baltic countries, where many Jews lived from the Middle Ages on, the most plentiful sweet fruit

was the apple, so apples became the traditional Rosh Hashanah fruit. But in places like Hungary and Austria, the Jews used plums more often than apples for Rosh Hashanah. This was because Italian plums came into season right before the holidays.

The apple is a member of the rose family. It is now the most widely cultivated fruit on the planet. Though the US is a big apple-growing country, China actually grows over five million more apples every year.

Lots of apples are good for making applesauce: Cortland, Gala, Golden Delicious (but not Red Delicious), Granny Smith, Pink Lady, Rome, Macintosh, Braeburn, Fuji.

Counting Eggs

"The eggs are wiser than the hens."
—Jewish saying

A young yeshiva student named Chaim went into a restaurant and had a simple breakfast of a single poached egg. But when it came time to pay, he realized he had no money with him.

"I'll pay as soon as I can," he told the owner, a miserly man named Tummler. "I study with Rabbi Shimmel."

Well, Master Tummler knew Rabbi Shimmel—who didn't?—and it was, after all, only a single egg. So he let the student go with a finger shake and thought no more of it. If he expected anything, it was that he would be paid the next morning. No—that was the Sabbath. Well, he would be paid the day after that. Yeshiva students were good customers, after all.

Chaim went back to the yeshiva and ate Sabbath eve dinner with the family where he was staying. The next morning he went to shul. And as young men do, he completely forgot about that egg.

In fact he forgot about it for years. He traveled with Rabbi Shimmel from Minsk to Pinsk to Moscow and beyond, becoming a great teacher himself. With Rabbi Shimmel, he taught in schools across the Pale, and even once in Paris.

Then one day, when Rabbi Shimmel was very old and frail and ready to return to his hometown, Chaim remembered that egg.

"Rabbi, I have a long-forgotten debt to pay," said Chaim. "Will you come with me and see that I repay it with grace and good will?" He knew the rabbi was worried that age had robbed him of his sharp wit. *Perhaps,* Chaim thought, *this will give him back some of his old confidence.*

Rabbi Shimmel nodded. "And we will have a good meal at the same time."

They found the restaurant and, amazingly, it was still open. The old owner's son was running it, but Master Tummler sat in the corner by the hearth, a bit stouter, a bit grayer, a bit bitter at being old.

Chaim and Rabbi Shimmel sat down and ordered a meal of boiled beans. No sooner had the beans been served than Master Tummler came over.

"Rabbi Shimmel," he said, "I never expected to see you in this life again."

The rabbi smiled. "In this life and the next," he said, nodding. "We old men must stick together. But my student here has something to say to you." He gestured to Chaim, who no longer looked like a student because he was a grown man now, with a full beard and even some gray at the temples.

Chaim shook hands with old Tummler, and said, "Sir, I owe you an apology. As a youth, I ate here often, and one time I had a meal of a single egg and not the money to pay for it. I promised to come back and to do so as soon as possible. To my shame, it has been twenty-five years, but here I am. What do I owe?"

Old Tummler looked at Chaim in a measuring way. This was no longer a callow yeshiva boy, but a man of substance. Surely there was money to be made. He sat down heavily.

"Let me see ..." he began. "A single egg, you say. But if I hadn't served you that single egg, it could have been born a chick. And that chick might have fathered ten chicks the next year. And each of them produce ten more chicks the next, not to mention extra eggs for me to serve to starving young students. Twenty-five years of eggs and chicks later, I would have made the sum of ..." And he named a number so vast that Chaim's jaw dropped.

"I see, I see," said Rabbi Shimmel, toying with his spoon. "You reason fairly as always, Tummler. So may I have you send over your son so we can work out this reasonable sum?"

Smelling a huge profit, Tummler went at once to fetch his son and brought him, along with his daughter-in-law, to the table. Smelling a story, all the people waiting for their own meals came to the rabbi's table as well.

"First," said the rabbi to the daughter-in-law, "would you take these beans outside and plant them for me? I want to gain the profit from all the trees that grow so we can pay your father-in-law his just sum." He handed her the bowl.

"But, Rabbi," she said, clearly laughing at him, "these beans have been boiled. They won't grow *anything* anymore."

"Hah!" said Rabbi Shimmel, one finger raised, "and neither will a boiled egg hatch a chicken. Come now, Master Tummler, what is the charge for a single boiled egg?"

Everyone applauded and said what a Solomon the old rabbi was.

As for Chaim, he had known this all the time.

THE FOUR VERSIONS I FOUND OF THIS STORY *were in Ellen Frankel's* The Classic Tales: 4,000 Years of Jewish Lore, *Peninnah Schram's* Jewish Stories One Generation Tells Another, *Sheldon Oberman's* Solomon and the Ant and Other Jewish Folktales, *and Matilda Koen-Sarano's* Folktales of Joha, Jewish Trickster.

Frankel's telling takes place in King David's court, where a servant is the one who eats the egg and the boy Solomon helps in the judgment. Schram's takes place in more modern times with Motl, a cart driver somewhere in Russia who goes to America and becomes a rich man. A young woman is the one who solves the problem. In Oberman's version— which takes place in an Eastern European shtetl—*the base story is crossed with Aesop's milkmaid tale. In the Koen-Sarano story, set in the Middle East, Joha is the one who teaches a Muslim judge a thing or two about eggs and wisdom. I chose to set the story in the Middle European Pale, starring a Jewish student and an old rabbi, who solves the problem.*

This story is Tale Type AT 821B, *"Chickens from Boiled Eggs," and is found throughout the Middle East, the Caucasus, and in many Mediterranean countries. It has also been used by lecturers in economics and accountancy.*

Shakshuka

Shakshuka is a breakfast food that is hearty enough for a full meal. Though you may not have seen it before, it is pretty common in Israel. The eggs can be prepared many ways, but my family likes them fully cooked. If you have leftovers, shakshuka is great the next day, too. Just heat the leftover tomato mixture and crack another egg (or two) into the pan.

MAKES 4 SERVINGS

INGREDIENTS

3	cloves garlic
1	onion
1	sweet pepper (any color)
4	large (or 6 small) Roma tomatoes
35	oz can tomatoes (whole peeled)
2	tbsp oil
1½	tsp paprika
1	tsp turmeric
1	tsp salt
½	tsp pepper
4	eggs

EQUIPMENT

- cutting board
- sharp knife
- can opener
- cup
- large heavy skillet (cast iron is best, but not necessary) with lid
- large spoon or spatula
- measuring spoons

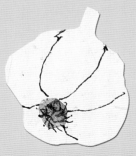
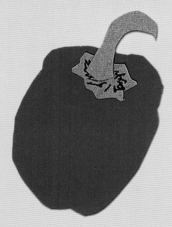

40

1. Prep the vegetables: Peel and chop the garlic and onion. Remove all the seeds and white insides from the pepper, and chop into medium-sized pieces. Chop the Roma tomatoes into large pieces.

2. Open the can of tomatoes and drain the juice into a cup to reserve for later, if needed. Chop the tomatoes into large pieces.

3. Put the oil, onion, and garlic into the large skillet and sauté, stirring often, for about 3 minutes on medium-low heat, until they look shiny and see-through, but not brown.

4. Add the fresh tomatoes and chopped pepper to the skillet and cook for 5 minutes, stirring frequently to make sure nothing burns or sticks to the bottom.

5. Add the canned tomatoes and all the spices (paprika, turmeric, salt, and pepper) to the skillet, bring to a boil, then lower the heat and cook for 30 minutes, stirring occasionally. (If the liquid all cooks off from the tomato mixture, you can add a little of the reserved tomato juice or water.)

6. Make a small indentation in the tomato mixture in the skillet (the liquid will fill it in, but the hole will still be there) and crack an egg carefully into the indentation. Do this for each egg. Repeat this step for each person eating so everyone has an egg.

7. Increase the heat so the tomato mixture is bubbling a bit, and cook for another 5–15 minutes, until the eggs set. You will see them turn white. The cooking time depends on how you like your eggs:

—For sunny side up, look for a light white cover to the yolk.

—If you prefer your yolk a bit more cooked, but still runny, make sure that the whole yolk is covered with opaque white.

—If you want your yolk solid, you can break the yolk once it is in the skillet, and stir it around lightly with a fork.

8. Season with salt and pepper to taste, and serve with bread—pita, toast, corn bread, naan, or whatever you like best.

VARIATIONS: *For quick shakshuka, you can use just canned tomatoes, omitting the peppers and Roma tomatoes.*

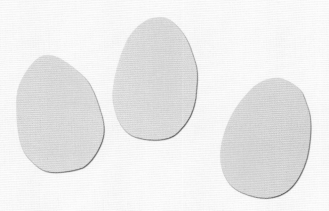

SHAKSHUKA IS A NORTH AFRICAN DISH—ORIGINALLY CHAKCHOUKA, *which is a Berber word for "vegetable ragout" or stew, or occasionally translated as "all mixed up."*

The dish was first enjoyed by the ruling classes of the Ottoman Empire and only later became a favorite of the masses. It is eaten throughout the Middle East, where it is not just a breakfast meal.

These days shakshuka (Hebrew for "to shake it all up") is the most popular egg dish in Israel.

The Demon Who Lived in a Tree

"Nothing is certain but death and blintzes."
—OLD JEWISH COMEDY ROUTINE

Long ago in old Germany, there lived a rabbi's son, Levi, who was a delightful child with dark curls and a loving heart. One evening Levi was playing outside with his best friend, David. David was hiding and Levi was seeking.

Seeing a hand half-hidden in the bole of the big tree outside his father's house, and believing it to be David's, Levi took off his ring and put it on the ring finger of the hand. Then, laughingly, he pronounced the wedding vows that he had so often heard his father perform.

Suddenly, the hand was pulled back into the tree. A moment later a grown woman peered out, grinning wickedly, her teeth yellow and pointed. She whispered in a harsh voice, "Mine!"

Levi didn't know if she meant the ring belonged to her or that he did. He screamed and ran off home, David galloping after him. Levi never told anyone exactly what had happened. As for his ring, he said that he'd lost it. Since he was a good boy, everyone believed him.

Levi grew into a fine young man. If he remembered the woman in the tree, it was only in his nightmares. Indeed, even he came to believe he had simply lost his ring in the woods.

On Levi's wedding day, the whole village was invited, since he was the rabbi's only son. And that night, after the ceremony, his bride—the daughter of a rabbi in a neighboring town—lingered outside her new home while Levi and his parents went inside. She walked over to a big tree and placed her hand on the trunk. The moment she did that, a woman emerged from the tree, grinning wickedly with yellowed teeth. She pulled back a branch and let it go. It snapped back, striking the new bride in the head, killing her instantly. Then the woman disappeared back into the tree.

There were tears, of course. Then more tears. Then a year of mourning. But accidents do happen. No one was to blame.

When the year of mourning was over and the yahrzeit candle lit, Levi was betrothed again to a girl from a village on the other side of the river. But on the night of this wedding, the same thing happened again. Levi's young bride was found at the foot of the tree, just like the first.

This time, along with the tears, there were mutterings that Levi was cursed. One new bride—an accident. But two? Not good at all.

"Papa," Levi said to his father, the rabbi. "Perhaps I *am* cursed."

"Then God will un-curse you," his father said. "For you have done nothing wrong."

But suspicion hung over Levi like a dark cloud. None of the local families would let him marry their daughters after that, even though he was the son of their rabbi and studying to become a rabbi himself.

A few years passed—lonely years for Levi—and at last a bride was found for him. Her name was Leah, and she was the youngest daughter of a poor man, so poor that he had no dowry or bride price. But Levi didn't care. Leah was a beautiful, modest, hard worker who was also very wise. And she was willing to marry him, cursed or not.

The wedding was arranged and then performed. And Leah—knowing what had happened to the first two brides—went outside carefully to look at the tree under which her two predecessors had died. But she was quick-witted and quick-footed as well. Noting that a branch was being drawn back by some unseen hand, she ducked, and it passed harmlessly over her head. Only then did she see the mysterious woman, her evil face surprised by how the girl had avoided her trap.

Leah followed the evil woman around the tree until she could see where the woman slipped back into a bole that was now quite far up the trunk.

"A curse ... or a demon?" Leah whispered to herself and went back into the house to explain to Levi exactly what she had seen.

"Then, it was no dream!" he blurted out, and told his new bride of the hide-and-seek game, and about the ring. "But why does she harm my wives, and not me?"

"Dearest," said Leah, putting her hands on his, "because she considers herself your bride. After all, even though it was in jest, you *did* give her a ring and say the wedding vows."

Levi turned pale. "Then we must burn down that cursed tree."

Leah shook her head. "No, my husband, that tree is her home. If you do that to her, she might do the same to you in return."

Levi began to pace back and forth. "What to do? What to do?"

Finally, Leah said to him, "Stop pacing and listen to what I propose."

So he sat down next to her and held her hands up to his heart.

"Demons love jam above all else," she said. "Perhaps I may make peace with your demon bride using jam."

"You must be careful."

"It is my middle name."

"It is?"

She laughed, a lovely sound, like small bells ringing.

. . . .

The very next day, Leah took a bowl of jam and put it at the bottom of the tree, on the side nearest the bole. Then she quickly, carefully, made her way back to the house.

The next morning when she went to retrieve the bowl, it was empty—except for a golden coin.

Ah, Leah thought, *a peace offering,* and brought it to Levi.

. . . .

Every day for almost a year, first thing in the morning, Leah left fresh-made jam in a bowl for the demoness. And every evening there was an empty bowl with a gold coin. Three hundred days, three hundred gold coins.

"I am grateful for the coins," said Levi, "but she is still a demon and not to be trusted."

And then, on the 301st day, Leah found out that she was with child. She told Levi, "Demonesses are often the daughters of Lilith, who strangles babies in their cradles. This child of ours is in danger. I must get the demon to promise not to hurt any of our family."

"How will you manage that?" Levi asked.

She told him her plan.

. . . .

So Leah went to the tree with an extra helping of jam and called up to the demoness. "Come forth, my jam-loving demon friend, for I would speak with you."

A long silence ensued. And then a shrill, horrible voice called out, "What do you want, human? Aren't the gold coins enough?"

"Most generous and more than enough," said Leah. "But I've come to talk about the ring and your claim as my husband's wife."

The demoness suddenly appeared, long black hair almost veiling her angry face. "Ah, and what do you propose to do about *that*?"

"I am willing to share him with you as my namesake shared her husband with her own sister Rachel. But only if you will vow by your mother's black heart never to harm any one of our family, including any children we may have. If you so agree, then he will come to you for one hour a day, at sunset, except on the Sabbath."

"Done," said the demoness, holding out her hand, where a boy's ring sparkled on her little finger.

. . . .

For the seven years that followed, Levi was a free man for all but one hour a day, when he was enslaved to his demon wife. He cooked for her, beat her rugs, washed her floors. He even recited verses from the Torah to her. She never let him rest. And if that hour felt like a day, he didn't complain.

At the end of seven years, Levi came as usual to the tree at sunset, and there in the bowl, which usually held a gold coin—"My wages of sin," Levi used to tell Leah—was the gold ring he'd long ago placed on the demon's finger. He picked it up and ran back home.

"Leah," he cried to his wife, who was feeding their four lovely children, "she's left us for good."

"Or perhaps, for bad," Leah said, smiling, as the children burst into a song of thanksgiving and praise.

I found this story in Howard Schwartz's Lilith's Cave *anthology, in a bare-boned retelling. I have emphasized Leah's role even more. She is, after all, the true hero of the tale.*

Schwartz cites as his source a sixteenth-century Yiddish manuscript in the library at Trinity College, Cambridge, manuscript 136 #5, "The Story of Worms" (Worms being a town in Germany).

The story of a demoness (or a corpse) who believes a man has betrothed himself to her—or married her—can be found in a number of places in Europe and Russia.

Filmmaker Tim Burton made an animated film, The Corpse Bride, *which draws on some of the same basic themes.*

Blintzes

My mom loves blintzes so much, she has been known to scold the waiters at our favorite brunch restaurant when they are not on the buffet. More than once the waiters have gone into the kitchen especially for her and brought out the sweet dish that makes everyone in our blintze-loving family happy.

MAKES 12–14

INGREDIENTS

Batter:

3   eggs

1¼ cups milk

¾   cup all-purpose flour

2   tbsp melted butter

Filling:

4   oz cream cheese

15 oz (1 ¾ cups) ricotta

1   egg

¼   cup powdered sugar

Choose one: zest of 1 lemon or ½ tsp lemon extract or ½ tsp vanilla

Cooking and serving:

oil for pan

butter

fruit preserves

powdered sugar

EQUIPMENT

- measuring cups
- electric mixer, blender, or whisk to mix the batter
- electric mixer or large spoon to mix the filling
- 2 bowls
- lemon zester or measuring spoon
- plastic wrap
- medium frying pan
- large frying pan
- spatula
- 3 plates
- spoon
- baking dish
- microwave-safe bowl or small saucepan

Make the batter for the blintze "leaves," which are very thin crepe-like pancakes:

1. Measure and combine all the batter ingredients and mix well with an electric mixer or in a blender. This can be done with a whisk, but it's better when done by a machine.

2. Cover with plastic wrap and set aside to let the bubbles settle. The batter should be thin.

Make the filling:

3. Measure and mix all the ingredients. (Cook's hint: If using lemon zest instead of lemon extract, use a zesting tool—very carefully so as not to cut yourself—to remove only the yellow part of the lemon peel. The white part is called the pith and is sour.)

4. Cover the mixture with plastic wrap, and put it in the refrigerator.

Make the blintze leaves:

5. Pour a small amount of oil (vegetable or another cooking oil) into a medium-sized frying pan. (Cook's hint: use a paper towel to spread the oil very thin before turning on the heat, and then rub the plates with the oily paper towel to keep the blintze leaves from sticking.)

6. Heat the pan to medium heat.

7. Pour a little less than ¼ cup of batter into the pan, and swirl the pan around until the batter covers the bottom with no holes. This will take some practice and the first leaf is usually pretty ugly.

8. When the edges start to peel up (about 30 seconds), use a spatula to gently turn the leaf in the pan and cook the second side for 20-30 seconds more.

9. With the help of the spatula, turn out the leaf onto the first plate.

10. Repeat steps 7–9 until you have used up all the batter.

Make the blintzes:

11. Take the top blintze leaf and move it to the second plate. Scoop a spoonful of the cheese mixture onto the leaf.

12. Fold ⅓ of the leaf up from the bottom, over the cheese mixture. Fold in both sides, then roll top down into a totally closed pocket.

13. Set the filled blintze onto the third plate.

14. Repeat steps 11–13 until you have used up all the leaves and filling.

15. Preheat the oven to 350°F.

16. Butter the bottom of a baking dish.

17. Melt 1-2 tablespoons of butter in a large frying pan at medium high heat, and gently place the blintzes (in batches so they don't touch and so you have room to flip them) into the pan. Cook until golden brown on one side, then flip them to brown on the other side—about 2-3 minutes per side. Add more butter if needed.

18. Remove each blintze from the frying pan and place them side by side in the buttered baking dish.

19. Bake for 15 minutes.

20. Heat fruit preserves in a small pan on low heat or in the microwave.

21. Top the blintzes with the warm preserves and sprinkle with powdered sugar.

VARIATIONS: *You can serve any kind of fresh fruit or jam with blintzes. You can also, to make this recipe much easier, buy pre-made "leaves" (or crepes) in the grocery store.*

THE BLINTZE (PRONOUNCED *BLIN'SAH*) **IS A THIN,** *rolled and folded pancake/crepe filled with sweetened cheese (ricotta, cottage, or farmer's cheese are easiest to find). It is usually topped with applesauce, sour cream, honey, or warmed fruit jams.*

In Jewish families, blintzes are served almost any time, as breakfast or snacks, or even desserts. They are especially popular at the holiday Shavuot because dairy products are the usual fare then. They are also served at Hanukkah because blintzes can be fried in oil, and oil is an important part of the Hanukkah tradition.

The blintze originated in Russia, where it is also called a blin or blini. In Russia, these are served at wakes and certain Russian Orthodox Christian spring holidays because, before the blini is rolled, it is shaped like the sun. Popular Russian toppings include caviar and sour cream.

A variety of different kinds of flour can be used in making blintzes: wheat, potato, buckwheat, oat. Some cooks insist that potato flour makes the blintze lighter.

And the Matzo Was Still Warm

"Somehow there's always money for matzos and shrouds."
—Yiddish folk saying

Many years ago in the city of Mainz, there was a good man named Gershon who had a son called Jacob. When Gershon was very ill, he told his son, "Here is my dying wish."

Jacob bent down to hear, and his father whispered, "Never cross the River Danube."

Weeping, Jacob promised. "Never, father. Never." He meant it with all his heart.

But before the old man could explain why he had made such an odd wish instead of giving Jacob his blessing, he was gone. And Jacob was left weeping.

But Jacob *wanted* to cross the Danube. Gershon had a famous relative, Rabbi Judah the Pious, who lived across the Danube in the city of Regensburg. Rabbi Judah the Pious was known for hundreds of miles around for his great learning. It was said that Rabbi Judah knew all the secrets of the Torah, and Jacob desperately wanted to learn them. But being mindful of his father's dying wish, he wouldn't cross the Danube.

Several years went by. Jacob married a woman named Leilah, had a son he named Gershon after his dead father, and still Jacob did not go over the river to study with Rabbi Judah. Anger at his dead father now gnawed at his soul and Jacob mourned, not his father, but his own lost chances.

His wife saw the restlessness in him. His son heard him sigh daily.

At last, one day Jacob said to them, "Surely my father didn't mean I should stay on the one side forever." Then, kissing them goodbye, Jacob went across the Danube, breaking his promise and leaving the only home he had ever known.

The river was wild with foam. The boat was spun about like a dreidel at Hanukkah. Jacob was sick the whole way. But once across the river, he felt fine. Leaping off the boat, he hurried to Regensburg—a trip of several days—going as fast as he could until he got to Rabbi Judah's house.

The rabbi came out of his house, the wind tousling his gray curls, and said to Jacob, "I should not greet you at all since you have disobeyed your father's dying wish that you never cross the Danube."

Wasn't Jacob surprised at that, for no one—*no one*—had been there when he had promised his father to stay at home. Surely the rabbi was a miracle worker. Or at least a mind reader. Either way, Jacob was impressed.

The rabbi continued, "But since you disobeyed in order to study Torah, I will greet you with kindness. Shalom."

And so Jacob joined the other young men who were studying with the rabbi.

He stayed one year. Two years. Three years. He wrote weekly to his wife and child. But he didn't go back home. He was waiting to learn the great secrets that Rabbi Judah knew. But all the rabbi taught was the simple meaning of the Torah and how to carry out the commandments.

First Jacob grew sorry for himself and then angry at the rabbi. "I've been away from my beautiful wife and my wonderful son for three years with little to show for it," he told himself, pacing up and down in his room. "Nothing but an aching heart and an empty mind."

At last it was the eve of Passover. Alone in his room, Jacob began to weep. "I should be at home, sitting at the head of my own table. My little boy would be asking the Four Questions. And I would tell him the story of how the Jews left Egypt." But then he gave himself a shake. He *had* learned something in those three years after all. "It's not the rabbi's fault. It's not my father's fault. This is *my* fault. I should never have disobeyed my father's dying wish."

He went to the dining room, where many of the young scholars were getting ready for the seder, the Passover meal.

Rabbi Judah came over to him. "I see you are troubled, my son, and sad. I know you wish you were back with your wife and son, listening to your boy asking the Four Questions."

Once again, the rabbi's miraculous mind-reading ability astonished Jacob. "I do indeed wish that, Rabbi," he admitted. "But it's already Passover Eve, and I could not reach Mainz until after the holiday. So it's a sadness with no cure."

The rabbi smiled and stroked his beard. "Ah, but what would you give me if I could get you home in time for the seder?"

Jacob laughed bitterly. "Must you make fun of me, Rabbi?"

"God forbid," Rabbi Judah rejoined. "I am being quite serious."

Then Jacob realized that Rabbi Judah would never have made fun of him, and answered, "I'd give you everything I possess."

"I would never ask for that," Rabbi Judah said. He took Jacob by the elbow and steered him toward the kitchen. "But it is getting late. Let us help bake the matzo. It only takes eighteen minutes, you know. After that, we will see what I can arrange to get you home."

Now, this truly puzzled Jacob. He knew that after they baked the matzo, they would sit down to dinner. And then after the seder, they would go to sleep. A Jew never travels on a holiday. *Nothing* the rabbi said made sense. But he decided to humor the old man.

In the kitchen, Jacob helped the baker while Rabbi Judah walked all around, inspecting the utensils, making sure everything that evening was being done according to the kosher laws.

When the last of the matzo came out of the oven, Rabbi Judah handed it to Jacob, wrapped in a napkin. "Take this, my son, and put it in your pocket. When you get home across the Danube, give it to your wife. It will still be warm."

Jacob did as the rabbi instructed.

"And now," the rabbi said, "while the table is being finished and all prepared for the seder, let us—you and I—take a walk outside in the fields."

Stranger and stranger, thought Jacob. But he was glad to have this chance to walk with his teacher. For even though he longed to be home with his wife and son, Jacob knew he'd miss the old man terribly if he left. It no longer mattered that he'd never been taught the great secrets.

Rabbi Judah put his hand on Jacob's shoulder. "I know you had hoped to learn all the secrets of the Torah. But you had disobeyed your father's dying wish. Still, you have been studying hard all these years, and so I will give you something."

He wrote some holy words in the sand with a stick. As Jacob read them, his mind and heart filled with wonder, for these were the very secrets he had longed for.

Rabbi Judah rubbed out the words with his hand and poured fresh sand over the place where the words had been. Immediately Jacob forgot everything he had just known.

Once again, and then a third time, Rabbi Judah did the same thing, then erased the words. And each time Jacob laughed with the knowledge and wept when it was taken from him.

But the fourth time, the rabbi said, "Bend down, my son, and lick the words from the sand. Take them into your mouth. Swallow them."

Jacob did as he was told, and this time the words became part of him, and from then on he didn't forget a single bit of that great knowledge.

When he stood, Jacob saw that the sun was ready to sink behind the horizon. At that same moment, Rabbi Judah put his hands on Jacob's head, whispering the blessing that Jacob's father had never given him. "Go in peace, my boy."

Jacob closed his eyes for the blessing. A breeze blew about his hair. And when he opened his eyes again, he found himself standing in front of his little house in Mainz.

Entering the house, he greeted his wife, who was even lovelier than before. His little son, almost four years old, looked up at the stranger with love in his eyes.

"Wife," Jacob said, handing her the matzo, "here is a gift from Rabbi Judah the Pious."

She took the matzo from him, unwrapped the napkin, and said with wonder in her voice, "Just feel it—it is still warm from the oven. How can that be?"

"A miracle," said Jacob. "But no more a miracle than this child of ours. Or the love between us. Or the love of Torah."

And they sat down to eat together as if no time had passed since Jacob had last been in their house.

I FOUND ONLY ONE TELLING OF THIS STORY, *in* A Golden Treasury of Jewish Tales, *retold by Asher Barash and translated from the Hebrew by Murray Roston. However, tales of miracle-working rabbis can be found throughout the Middle European countries. Was this supposed to be a dream that Jacob had? Or was it a true miracle? You can read the story either way.*

The Danube is the second longest river in Europe, after the Volga. It flows through or forms part of some ten countries, including Germany, Austria, Slovakia, Hungary, Croatia, Bulgaria, Moldova, Romania, Serbia, and the Ukraine.

Mainz is a very old city (over 2,000 years old) in Germany. Regensburg is located on the confluence of the Danube and Regen Rivers. It is a university town.

Matzo Brei

A battle rages over matzo brei. Though most people will tell you their way is the only way to cook it, the good news is that there is no wrong way. Experiment with this recipe. My family likes it omelet-style, with maple syrup.

SERVES 2

INGREDIENTS

water

4   sheets of matzo

3   large eggs

pinch of salt

pinch of pepper

butter or oil for the pan

EQUIPMENT

- two bowls
- fork
- whisk (optional)
- medium frying pan (a sauté pan with vertical sides is best)
- spatula

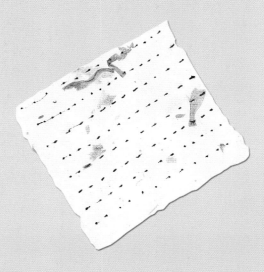

1. Fill a bowl with water halfway.

2. Break the matzo into pieces, and drop into the water.

3. While the matzo is soaking, break the eggs into a second bowl, add the salt and pepper, and whisk them (or beat with a fork).

4. Take handfuls of the soggy matzo out of the water, and squeeze them with your hands over the sink to drain. Drop the matzo into the egg mixture, and grab another handful of matzo. Do this until all the soggy matzo is in the eggs.

5. Mix with a fork to break up the balls of matzo.

6. Heat butter or oil in the pan on medium heat, and pour in the matzo and egg mixture, spreading it out evenly with a fork.

7. Cook until it is mostly dry on the top and holds together in one piece (about 3 minutes), then carefully slide the spatula under the entire thing, and flip. If you are not quite brave enough to attempt this, you can cut it into pieces before flipping.

8. Cook another 2 minutes.

9. Lift out onto a plate, cut, and serve with either salt and pepper for a savory meal, or cinnamon sugar, syrup, jam, or honey if you prefer it sweet.

VARIATIONS: *You can make matzo brei like scrambled eggs—just stir it with a spatula while cooking, instead of letting it set in one big piece. Try changing the egg-to-matzo ratio. Some people soak the matzo in water first (as I do), but others put it straight into the eggs.*

MATZOH OR MATZAH OR MATZO? *Since the word itself has to be transliterated from the Hebrew characters, there is no absolutely right way to write the name.*

There is nothing besides flour and water in matzo. Not even salt. It sustains life but has no coloring or flavoring to enhance the act of eating.

Matzo is considered the centerpiece of the Passover Seder, the holiday that celebrates the time when Jews escaped from enslavement in Egypt. As they fled Egypt—so the Torah tells us—the Jews had to move so quickly, they had no time to let the bread rise. So unleavened bread— lechem oni, which means "bread of poverty" or "bread of our affliction"—became the symbol of that exodus. Matzo is also called "the bread of faith."

All over the world, for the eight days of Passover, Jews forgo any food that is baked with yeast, which is the ingredient that makes bread rise.

That means no cakes, cookies, pasta, or noodles. Jews also scour their houses to get rid of any crumbs that would compromise the celebration.

In 1838, a Frenchman named Isaac Singer invented a matzo-dough-rolling machine that made mass production possible. In 1888, the first matzo-making factory was built—the B. Manischewitz Company in Cincinnati, Ohio. There, an entirely automated method of matzo production was started. Manischewitz ran ads boasting, "No human hand touches these matzos!" These days, there are companies that produce flavored matzo, organic and gluten-free matzo, even spiced matzo and matzo covered in chocolate.

Matzo brei is a dish that uses broken bits of matzo, and is commonly served at Passover. Matzo brei has been called "Jewish French toast" and is eaten with all kinds of toppings: jelly, jam, cinnamon, maple syrup, brown sugar, apple butter—the list is endless.

The Loaves in the Ark

"If you look only for challah, you lose the black bread."
—JEWISH SAYING

Way back in the sixteenth century, in the town of Safed in Ottoman Palestine, lived the great Rabbi Isaac Luria, known by all as the Holy Ari. People came from far and near to study Torah with him.

One particular couple traveled all the way from Portugal to be with Holy Ari and to return to the faith of their ancestors. Like many other Marranos, or Sephardic (Hispanic) Jews, they'd been forced to become Christians. So they sold all that they had and made the long trip. But as great as their desire to be Jewish was, they knew little about Judaism. They often got things wrong. Still they learned and kept on learning.

Now one day, the husband was at shul and heard the rabbi giving a sermon about what he called *shewbread,* which the rabbis in old Jerusalem used to offer at the temple on every Sabbath. It was sifted thirteen times, baked with noble thoughts, and then brought to the ark of the Torah in the hopes of pleasing the Lord.

"But," the rabbi said with a great sigh of resignation, "shewbread is not offered anymore. Not since the destruction of the Temple."

When the Marrano heard this, it was as if a shaft of light had entered his heart. He rushed home and told his wife that they must make an offering of two loaves of shewbread. Delighted to be able to demonstrate their adherence to Jewish custom, his wife immediately set to baking the twisted challah for that Sabbath, two loaves for themselves and two extra loaves—lovingly sifted, kneaded, and blessed—for the synagogue.

She wrapped the two loaves in a scarf she'd made. Then, before evening services, the Marrano took the loaves and placed them in front of the ark, saying, "If it pleases thee, Lord, take this shewbread as our offering. May it remind thee of the time when we Jews were in Jerusalem. May the bread—and the memory— be sweet in thy mouth."

After, he left to wash his hands and make himself ready for evening prayers.

No sooner had the Marrano left the shammash came to work. His first job was to clean the floor around the ark. And there he discovered the scarf and its precious gift of two still-warm Sabbath loaves.

Now, the shammash and his large family were very poor, and they'd never had two whole loaves of challah for their Sabbath meal. So he thought, "Some generous soul has left this gift for us and wants to be anonymous. Thank you, dear Lord, for this." He took the bread home and his family had their best Sabbath meal ever.

So it went for many months, the Marrano and his wife baking the bread and thinking that God had taken it up to Heaven and eaten it, the shammash and his family grateful for their benefactor's gift. Both rejoiced in what they considered a great miracle.

But one Friday, the shewbread rabbi came early to finish writing his sermon and was working behind the lectern. He was crouched over his papers, so the Marrano did not see him.

Setting the two loaves of challah at the door of the ark, the Marrano said as always, "If it pleases thee, Lord, take this shewbread as our offering. May it remind thee of the time we Jews were in Jerusalem. May the bread—and the memory—be sweet in thy mouth." Then he turned to leave.

The rabbi stood, shaking with fury. "You idiot! You foolish man! Do you really think that the Lord eats with a human mouth or tastes with a human tongue? What a sin to think that way. You shame the Lord, you shame the Torah. You shame this congregation. You shame *me*. It is someone else who has been taking your offering, probably the shammash."

The Marrano, who but moments before had been filled with the light of Heaven, hung his head. Of course, he saw it now: he *was* a fool. And a sinner, as well.

Just then the shammash came in and the rabbi began to question him.

The shammash, too, hung his head. "Yes, Rabbi, I took the loaves. I thought they were left as a *mitzvah*, a gift, for one in need. All these weeks my family has had a happy Sabbath with the miracle of these loaves. But I see that I, too, have been a sinner."

At that very moment, a messenger came into the sanctuary. "I have a message," he said to the rabbi, "from the Holy Ari."

The rabbi turned eagerly. The Holy Ari rarely sent messages to the other rabbis. Surely this was a good thing.

The messenger looked at him severely. "My Master says that you must go home at once and set your house in order, for tomorrow you will die. So Heaven wills it."

Forgetting sermon, sinners, and all, the rabbi hurried to the house of the Holy Ari. "Why do you send me such a message?" he demanded.

Holy Ari put his finger into his book to mark the page where he was studying Midrash. His face was stern. "You will die for depriving the Lord of one of his greatest pleasures. After the temple fell in Jerusalem and shewbread was no longer left as an offering the Lord had little pleasure in his people. And then the Maranno and his wife began leaving shewbread, which went to serve a family who had so little, and this became a great pleasure to the Lord. Now you have not only stopped the gift, but humiliated both men, so you have been condemned to die."

The rabbi, realizing how greatly he had sinned, went home and set his affairs in order. The next day, at the very time he would have been giving his sermon, he died.

A Marrano is a Sephardic (Hispanic/Portuguese) *Jew forced to adopt Christianity under threat of execution or exile, but who practiced Judaism in secret. This meant there was much about being Jewish that a Marrano would not know.*

There are many versions of this story. I found four of them in books by Ellen Frankel, Yisroael Klapholtz, Howard Schwartz, and Pinhas Safer.

A Jewish house of worship is called a synagogue or temple or shul. The Torah—the scroll on which the entire Bible is written in Hebrew—is kept in an ark, which is an ornate storage container/closet on a raised dais known as the bimah *at the front of the synagogue.*

The shammash (also spelled shamash or shammas) comes from the Hebrew word for servant. He is employed by the synagogue to do everything from secretarial work to janitorial duties. A rabbi is an ordained teacher who has studied both the Hebrew Bible and Talmud. He may also be the religious leader of the synagogue.

Challah

I have two confessions to make. First, I don't love baking. I love cooking, which is experimenting with ingredients and trying new things. But baking is an exact science. So I am always looking for shortcuts in baking. My favorite is a food processor. But this whole recipe can also be made by hand if you don't have a food processor. My second confession is that my challah never looks very pretty. No one would want to photograph it for a fancy culinary magazine. But I promise it tastes great. And when it comes to food, isn't that the most important part?

This recipe makes one loaf of challah. The traditional way to make it is in two loaves. So if you want to make two, just double the recipe.

INGREDIENTS

- ½ cup warm water
- 1 envelope active dry yeast (2¼ tsp)
- 1 tsp sugar
- 2 tbsp honey
- 1 tbsp oil
- 1 tbsp sugar
- 1 tsp salt
- 1 egg
- 2 to 2½ cups all-purpose flour
     oil
- 1 egg
     cooking spray (optional)

EQUIPMENT

- measuring cup
- measuring spoons
- large bowl or food processor with metal blade
- timer
- 2 small bowls
- spoon for mixing
- board or clean counter space
- large bowl for rising
- plastic wrap
- clean cloth (optional)
- knife
- baking sheet
- basting brush

1. Put the water, yeast, and 1 teaspoon sugar in the bowl of a food processor or a large bowl, and set the timer for 10 minutes.

2. While you wait, combine the honey, oil, 1 tbsp sugar, and salt in a small bowl, then add the egg.

3. When the timer dings, add the honey mixture to the yeast mixture.

4. Mix using the food processor (or a spoon) until blended together.

5. Pour flour into the wet mixture a little at a time, mixing in each batch before adding more. When a ball forms, add a little more flour, and mix, remembering that you don't have to use all the flour and you can always add more.

6. Sprinkle flour on a clean countertop or a board, and remove the dough from the processor (the blade is like a knife, so be careful not to touch it), or bowl. Knead the dough by hand on the floured surface for about ten minutes.

7. Pour a teaspoon of vegetable or any light cooking oil into the large bowl, and put the ball of dough into it. Cover the bowl with plastic wrap or a wet (but not dripping) towel, and place the bowl aside to rise. Set the timer for 90 minutes.

8. When the dough has risen for 90 minutes, take a small handful of flour and sprinkle it on the board or counter. Uncover the dough and punch it down with your fist a couple of times. Then put it on the floured surface, and pull or roll it into a fat rope.

9. Cut the dough into 3 equal pieces then roll and pull those pieces into three thinner ropes.

10. Braid the dough: Take 2 dough ropes and lay them out in an X shape. Lay the third horizontally on top of them, so all three intersect in the middle. Starting from the middle and working with the three pieces on the right, lift the top right piece and place it between the two. Then lift the lower right piece and place it between the upper two. Repeat this braiding until you get to the end of that side. Squish the three ends together and tuck them under. Start again at the middle and work the same way toward the left.

11. Grease the baking sheet with a little oil or cooking spray, and set the challah loaf on it. Cover lightly with plastic wrap, set the timer, and let it rise again for 60 minutes.

12. Heat oven to 350°F.

13. After 60 minutes, in a small bowl, mix a beaten egg with a little water, brush onto the top of the challah, then put the loaf in the oven to bake for 30–35 minutes.

14. When the challah is done, it should be golden brown and make a hollow sound when the bottom is tapped.

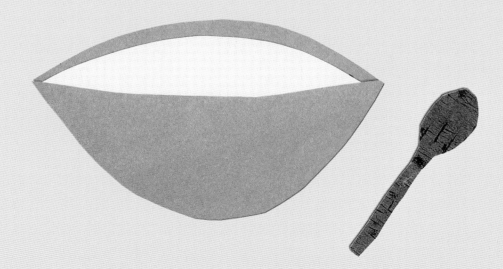

VARIATIONS: *After you brush the challah with egg wash, you can lightly press sesame or poppy seeds into the top of the loaf or sprinkle it with cinnamon sugar. Or try kneading raisins into the dough at the end, just before you cut it into pieces.*

Challah can be made with 6 braided ropes. This is more complicated than the 3-rope variety. But if you are feeling ambitious, there are great videos online that demonstrate how to do this. If you want to make a circular challah for the New Year, when you are done braiding, bring the ends together and squish them until they connect.

If you have leftover challah, it makes the best French toast for the next day's breakfast.

CHALLAH, OR HALLAH, *is a special braided bread also known as* khale *in eastern Yiddish. Other names for challah are* barches *(German and western Yiddish),* bergis *(Sweden), and* kitke *(South Africa).*

The Sabbath eve (Friday night) and holiday eve meals all begin with a blessing over two loaves to remember the miracle of manna in the desert after the Israelites—under Moses' leadership—crossed the Red Sea and were starving in the desert. According to tradition, manna did not fall on the Sabbath or on holidays but a double portion fell on the eve before. Challah often has sesame or poppy seeds sprinkled on top, also symbolizing the manna falling down from Heaven.

While modern bakers use white or whole-wheat flour for challah, some bake in the old way, using "spelt," a European species of wheat used from the Bronze Age until the days of the Romans. Most challah is braided with six strands of dough to represent the six days of the week that led to the unifying seventh day, the Sabbath.

Some bakers set aside a small piece of the dough (called hafrashat challah, *from which the challah is named). This piece is separated*

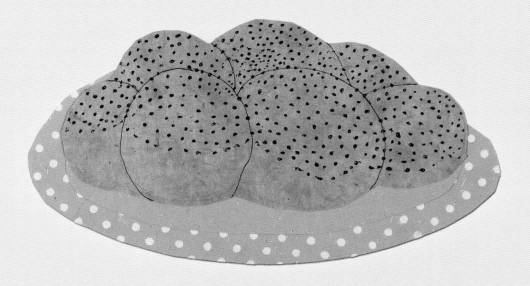

from the rest of the dough before the braiding. It is considered a tithe, or a voluntary contribution (usually a tenth) for the support of the priesthood, who—in the old days—had no other employment. These days that small piece is usually thrown into the fire.

Another custom with challah includes a circular bread baked especially for the eve of Rosh Hashanah, the Jewish New Year. It's a reminder that a year is circular, the end of the old year becoming the beginning of a new year. The top of this bread may be brushed with honey. People then say, "May you have a sweet new year."

In homes where families keep the Sabbath rituals, the challah is placed on a board and covered with a special cloth that represents the dew surrounding the manna in the desert. Though a more fanciful explanation comes from Joseph Caro, who wrote a code of Jewish law in the sixteenth century. He said that the bread is usually blessed first on normal days, then the wine. But on the Sabbath it is the other way around. So the bread needs to be covered on the Sabbath so as not to be "embarrassed."

The Wheat Came in at the Door

"There are no bagels west of Allen Street."
—LOWER MANHATTAN JEWISH SAYING

There was once a wheat dealer named Aron who was known for his charity. Though he was not a rich man, he gave to the poor without ever counting the cost.

Now, his daughter, the beautiful Devora, was about to be married, and Aron's wife sent him to the market to buy food for the wedding feast.

He also had in his pocket, carefully counted out, the money for his daughter's wedding dress and trousseau.

As Aron walked through the market, looking at the beets, holding up carrots and fish to the light to see if they were fresh enough for the bridal feast, the people at the market greeted him and wished him joy of the coming wedding day and grandchildren soon to follow.

But one woman, knowing his great charity, stopped him, saying, "While I wish you joy, Aron, there is an orphan on my street who is to be married on this very day. And she has nothing to wear for her wedding, and no dowry, either."

Aron did not even stop to think about it. He went right to the seamstress who was making the wedding dress for his daughter, and instead bought a dress for the orphan girl. Then he took the dress to the girl's house and led her to the wedding canopy. He gave his blessing (and a handsome dowry, too) as if he were her father.

Of course, because he was not a wealthy man, he had hardly a coin left for his own daughter's wedding. In order to make a little more money so that there might be *some* sort of feast, he used his last coin for a bit of wheat to sell. Then, after telling his wife what he'd done, he put the wheat into a cupboard and went off to the synagogue to pray.

When Aron came back from shul, he found his wife in the larder, hands on her hips, laughing and weeping at the same time.

"What's wrong?" he asked, putting his arms around her. "What has happened?"

"Look!" she told him. The cupboard door had burst open, and wheat was pouring out onto the floor. Much more wheat than a single coin could have bought. More than a bag of gold could have bought.

Aron and his wife danced and danced through the house. There was so much wheat to sell, they had enough for their daughter's wedding, dowry, and ...

"And *tzdekah*—charity!" Aron said.

Of course his wife, who knew him well and loved him well, agreed.

THIS IS A MUCH-BELOVED MIDRASH STORY. *Sometimes it is about a simple miller or a dealer in wheat, sometimes about a pious rabbi. But the miracle and moral are always the same.*

The Jewish people put great store in tzdekah—giving charity to those in need. Even the poor are told that giving charity is the surest way to please God. "Tzdekah is equal to all the other commandments combined," say the rabbis. The Hebrew word tzdekah *is commonly translated simply as charity, but it also has roots in the word for justice or fairness (tzdek).*

Weddings (and other special days) have always been times of special charity, and the bride and groom are supposed to give joyfully on their special day.

The famous twelfth-century rabbi, scholar, and philosopher Moses Maimonides wrote this about tzdekah: "There are eight levels of tzedakah each one higher than the other. The highest one of all is when one takes the hand of one from Israel and gives him a gift or a loan, or engages him in a partnership, or finds him work by which he can stand on his own and not require any charity. Thus it is written: "And you strengthened the stranger who lives with you." i.e. Strengthen him so he won't fall and need your help."

BAGELS

The difference between bagels and other bread is that bagels are boiled before they are baked. We love bagels at my house and eat them in all sorts of ways. The traditional way is toasted with a schmear of something yummy like cream cheese (me), butter (Glen), peanut butter (Maddison), or with cream cheese and lox (Nana). But to be honest, our favorite way to eat bagels in this house is as a sandwich with fresh mozzarella, tomato, and pesto, which, though not traditional, certainly shows the bagel's versatility.

MAKES 12 BAGELS

INGREDIENTS

¼ cup warm water

1 envelope active dry yeast (2¼ tsp)

1 tsp sugar

1¼ cup water

1 tbsp sugar

1 tsp salt

1 tbsp olive oil

4 cups all-purpose flour

oil (not olive)

flour

cooking spray (optional)

EQUIPMENT

- large bowl or food processor with a metal blade
- measuring cup
- measuring spoons
- kneading surface (stone countertop or a large smooth cutting board)
- large bowl
- plastic wrap
- knife
- large pot
- slotted spoon
- plate
- baking sheet(s)
- tongs or spatula

1. In a large bowl or in the bowl of a food processor, pour ¼ cup warm water. Add 1 package (or 2¼ teaspoon) yeast and 1 teaspoon sugar. Let this sit while you measure the other ingredients.

2. After 5 to 10 minutes, add the rest of the water, sugar, the salt and olive oil. Mix with the food processor or, if you are mixing by hand, with a spoon.

3. Start adding the flour in batches—about ½ cup at a time—mixing in each batch completely before adding more. If your dough seems too sticky, add a little more flour a teaspoon at a time.

4. Once all the flour is incorporated into the dough, take a small amount of flour, sprinkle it onto your clean surface, and rub your hands together to coat them with flour. Remove the dough (if you are using a food processor, remember that the blade is like a knife, so be careful not to touch it), and start kneading it on the floured surface. Use more flour on the surface and your hands if necessary. Knead for about 10 minutes.

5. Pour a small amount (a teaspoon should do) of vegetable or any light cooking oil into a bowl, put the ball of dough into it, turn it around a bit, and cover it with plastic wrap. Set aside for an hour.

6. After an hour, remove the plastic wrap (and set it aside), punch the dough, and put it back on the floured surface. Cut it into pieces by making three balls of dough and rolling each into a log. Cut the log in half and then in half again, until you have 12 pieces (or more, depending on the size of bagels you want).

7. Roll each piece into a thinner rope, and wrap it around to form a circle. Knead the ends together and press it down lightly to make a bagel shape. Your bagels will grow, so they should be smaller than you want your final bagels. Set them all aside, and place plastic wrap lightly over them.

8. Fill a large pot approximately halfway with water, and set it to boil on high heat. Let your bagels sit to rise again while the water comes to a boil.

9. Heat the oven to 425°F.

10. Remembering that the bagels will grow in size, drop the bagels in batches into the boiling water (careful not to splash) and count to 60. With tongs or a slotted spoon, turn over each bagel in the water, and count to 60 again. With a slotted spoon, remove each bagel and set it to dry on a plate. The slotted spoon works better than tongs for this step because boiled bagels are slippery.

11. When all the bagels are boiled, oil a cooking sheet (you can cover it with tin foil first), and place the bagels on it. Put it in the heated oven.

12. Bake for 10 minutes on one side, remove, and turn each bagel with tongs or a spatula. Bake another 10 minutes. Remove to cool.

ONE OF THE MOST ICONIC JEWISH FOODS IS THE LOWLY BAGEL. *It is a kind of bread made of wheat and shaped into the form of a hand-sized ring. It is first boiled for a short time in water, and then baked.*

Some food historians point to Krakow, Poland, as the place where bagels originated in the sixteenth century, though others say the first mention was in 1610. Possibly the bagels were cooked Saturday evening after the Sabbath was over, since cooking and other work is not allowed on the Day of Rest in strict Orthodox tradition, and bagels are very quick breads to make.

Bagels came into Britain and North American cuisine in the middle of the nineteenth century, as more Jews became citizens there. But when

VARIATIONS: *After boiling, try adding poppy seeds, sesame seeds, salt, or dried garlic. Or, while you are kneading the dough, add in cinnamon sugar for a sweeter bagel.*

Slice, and serve toasted, cold, on its own, or with just about any topping you can dream up.

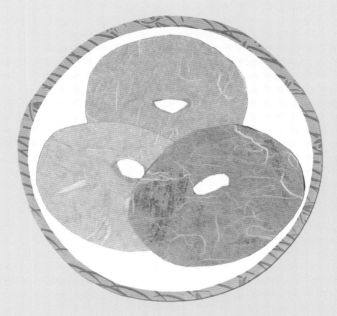

Harry and Florence Sender pioneered frozen bagels in the 1960s, bagels became beloved by non-Jews as well.

The name may have come from beugal, meaning bow or bale, or from the Yiddish beygl, which means ring, the shape of a bagel.

Ordinary bagels are either plain or have seeds (poppy and sesame) baked on top. But in the past forty years or so, the variety of bagels has grown enormously. Cinnamon raisin, onion, vegetable, jalapeno, garlic, baked apple, blueberry, sourdough, olive oil and rosemary, and sun-dried tomato are only a few of the new-style bagels. Oh yes—and chocolate chip!

❖ SOUP ❖

A Little Bit of Soup
Chicken Soup

The Flour Barrel and the Water Jug
Matzo Balls

A Little Bit of Soup

"Worries go down better with soup than without."
—Yiddish saying

There was once—though it hurts to tell of it—a great rabbi who was very rich but a terrible miser. *Ach, tu-tu-tu,* I spit through my fingers. But wait, good comes of this.

There was once a great rabbi who, though rich, was a terrible miser. To his wife—may she be blessed—he portioned out food using a short scale. And he never went over in his counting.

His wife said, "Husband, we must give food to the poor as well. Does it not say so in Scripture?"

"And what do you know of Scripture?"

So every day, when he went off to the shul—where everyone in the congregation praised his name—his wife would take a portion of her own soup and, without the rabbi's knowledge, put it in a bowl for the poor. This beggar's bowl she placed in a small window in the kitchen, and then she opened the window.

The smell would wind down the alleyway and always a beggar or a poor child or a mother in need would follow the smell and take the offering. And in this way, the rabbi's wife did a mitzvah every single day.

Now a terrible thing happened. The rabbi came home one afternoon—on the Sabbath, mind you—and the moment he stepped foot in the house, he fell over dead. *Ach, tu-tu-tu,* I spit through my fingers.

The wife cried. Of course she did. He may have been a miser, but was otherwise a good man. She sent the serving girl to the shul to tell everyone, and as soon as the Sabbath was over, they came.

They brought a coffin with them, not just a plain one—a fancy one—for the rabbi had been famous throughout the city. Meanwhile, the wife had the people in from the *Chevra Kadisha* to prepare the body for burial, because Jewish law says burial has to be as soon as possible.

But when the men tried to bring the coffin in the front door, it was too big and too fancy to go through. And when they tried to take it in the back door, that didn't work either.

"What shall we do?" the men asked.

Just then the wife spoke up, tears glistening in her eyes. "There is a small window in the kitchen," she said. "Try taking it through there."

They began to laugh at her. "Are you *meshugenah*, Mrs. Rabbi?" they said, meaning crazy, loco, no pickle on her sandwich.

"Please, *please* try it that way," she begged them.

So they marched the coffin around to the side of the house, and the rabbi's wife opened the small window—the one where she'd always put the little bit of soup for the poor.

Miracle of miracles—the window widened and widened and widened still further until it was large enough for the coffin and all six of the bearers to go through.

• • • •

The next day, after the rabbi was buried and the widow was sitting shiva in the house, the men of the shul came to pay her a visit with their wives. The wives brought cakes and kugel and rugalach and goodness knows what else. They were all very nervous and wanted to ask her what had happened with that window. But for the longest time they just sat in the parlor, passing the food around, their mouths so full, no one could actually talk.

Finally, the junior rabbi could take it no more. He downed a glass of wine and said, "Madam, we all want to know how come…"

Finally, the widow took a deep breath and started to speak. "It must be said that as great a rabbi as my husband was, he was also a miser, this you may not know."

The men and their wives looked at one another sheepishly. Actually, they knew quite a bit about his miserliness, so they just sat still.

"My husband measured every bit of my food, only so much and no more. But are we not commanded to help the poor?"

A few of the women nodded. Then the junior rabbi. And soon they were all nodding.

"So I kept a third from my own plate every day and gave it away to those in need, setting out the bowl in that kitchen window." The widow dabbed at her eyes with a hankie.

The men sat, wiping their mouths and nodding. The women leaned forward, and one touched the widow's knee. "There, there," she said.

"My husband, may the earth rest lightly upon him, did not know that I did this. But someone else did." The widow pointed a finger toward the heavens.

The men all muttered, "Yes, the Lord knew."

"And perhaps that is why He had me speak to you yesterday to take the coffin through the window. For it was not me speaking, but Him."

After that, everything the rabbi's widow undertook was golden. She became a rich woman in her own right and built great storehouses for food, which she gave away to those who needed it. And the more she gave away—well, the more she received.

Didn't I tell you good would come of this?

A MUCH SHORTER VERSION OF THIS STORY *can be found in Barbara Rush's* The Book of Jewish Women's Tales *(called "By Right of His Wife's Charity") and in A. Stahl's* Stories of Faith and Morals, *IFA #17.*

When the narrator in the story says tu-tu-tu, *she spits between the horns made when the point finger and pinkie are extended but the other fingers are bent in toward the palm. It is the old sign to ward off evil.*

Charity is so important in the Jewish faith that tales reminding (and warning) people to give generously are common.

According to Jewish tradition, a burial must take place within a day or two of a death, and usually in a simple pine box, though that is not necessarily done all the time. The Chevra Kadisha *is a society that prepares the dead for burial under strict laws—men prepare men, and women prepare women.*

Sitting shiva is a seven-day mourning period in which the deceased's family receives company for the week. Flowers are not sent to the house, but food is. Then there is a year's mourning, after which the family lights a yahrzeit candle in memory, and again at the anniversary of the death every year.

Chicken Soup

There are lots of soup rules: Don't let it boil, because it will cloud. Cover the pot. Don't cover the pot. Skim the fat. Don't skim the fat. I tend to ignore all these rules, throw everything in, and just cook the soup. No one ever complains, and I think it tastes just fine. Add matzo balls, some fresh dill, and it is perfect. Add noodles, pasta stars, or rice for a different soup. Have fun.

MAKES 6-8 SERVINGS

INGREDIENTS

chicken (uncooked—use whatever pieces and parts are available or the least expensive. Grab a couple of leg quarters and some wings or use a whole cut-up bird. You can also use leftover cooked chicken from the night before or a rotisserie chicken that's already cooked)

1–2 tsp salt

1 tsp pepper

2 large onions

5 large carrots

2 parsnips

5 celery stalks

3 garlic cloves

½ lemon

large handful of fresh herbs (whatever you have in your fridge, garden, or grocery store—you can even buy a "soup mix" of fresh herbs in the produce section)

fresh dill

EQUIPMENT

- measuring spoons
- large pot
- cutting board
- knife
- peeler (optional)
- slotted spoon
- tongs
- strainer and large bowl (optional)

1. Put the chicken into a large pot and sprinkle with salt and pepper.

2. Fill the pot with cold water up to the top of the chicken and then another inch or two. Set it on high to boil.

3. Prep the vegetables, herbs, and lemon: Cut the ends off the carrots, parsnips, and celery. Wash them and, if you want, peel the carrots and parsnips (I don't peel, because I like the texture better that way). Cut the ends off the onions but leave the skins on. Wash the lemon and cut it in half. Peel the garlic cloves. Remember, you can use these ingredients or any others in a chicken soup. No ingredient, except the chicken, is vital. Soup is about what *you* want in it.

4. Toss all the vegetables, half lemon, and the handful of herbs into the pot with the chicken. Bring to a boil, and lower the heat to simmer.

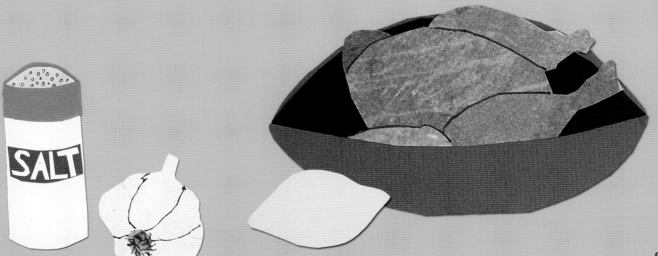

5. Cook for two or three hours (less if you are using already-cooked chicken). Check every once in a while and stir it around.

6. When the soup is done, let it cool a bit. Now you have to separate what you want in your soup from the stuff you do not. First, either remove everything from the broth with a slotted spoon and tongs, or pour off the broth by placing a strainer (colander) in a large bowl and pouring the entire pot slowly through the strainer. This will capture the broth in the bowl and the rest in the strainer. If you have used the strainer method, pour the broth back into the pot. Next, chop the chicken meat and the vegetables into bite-sized bits, and put them back into the pot with the broth. Discard the rest (the lemon half, the onion skin, the bones).

7. Sprinkle with fresh dill before serving.

8. Serve the soup with matzo balls, rice, noodles, pasta stars—or just as it is.

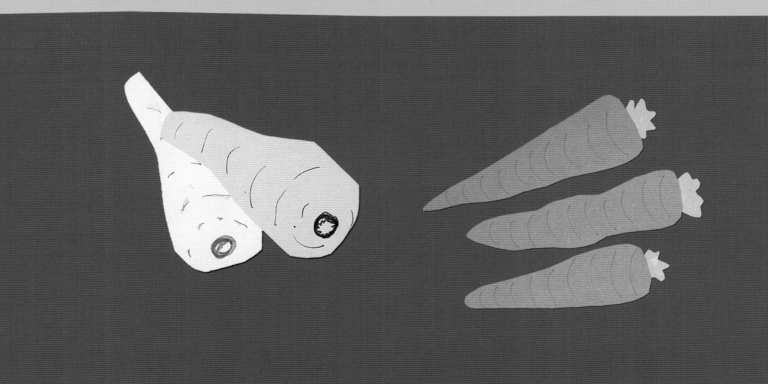

THE RABBI'S WIFE PROBABLY WOULD HAVE BEEN SHARING *one of the three most popular soups for Jews—chicken soup, matzo ball soup, or soup with kreplach—whichever she had made for the rabbi's dinner the night before. It's just as tasty the second and third day, as well.*

Chicken soup is supposed to cure all ills, but especially a cold or the flu. At least that's what folklore tells us. It's sometimes called "Jewish penicillin." The doctors say, "It couldn't hurt."

There are matzo balls that float, and heavier ones, called sinkers, that do just that. Sinkers have more matzo meal in them than the floaters.

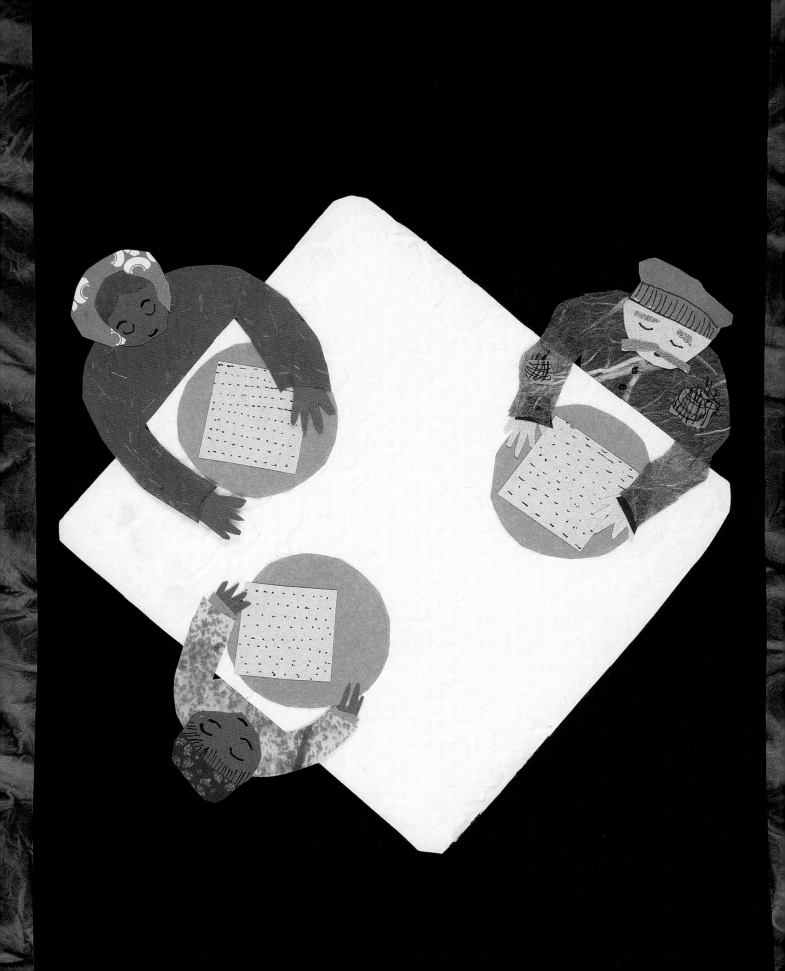

The Flour Barrel and the Water Jug

"Matzo is lechem oni, the bread of poverty."
—Torah

Long ago in Ancient Israel, there was a fierce drought. Even the little streams disappeared. Everyone prayed for rain, though no one prayed harder than the prophet Elijah, who had come to walk along the dry, dusty paths to see for himself how the people were suffering.

One morning he came upon a small house, barely two rooms, where a widow lived with her young son. The boy was outside, playing in the dirt with a straw, drawing fanciful ships on even more fanciful rivers. His mother watched him from the window.

Elijah stopped, nodded at the boy, and spoke to the widow. "Do you have a cup of water for a desperately thirsty traveler?"

Though the woman had but a small jug of water left, she immediately poured the traveler a cup.

Elijah smiled. "And could you, perhaps, spare me a bit of bread?"

"Oh my poor man, I would if I could. But it is Pesach—Passover—and the house has been swept clean of all crumbs. I have just a little bit of spelt and the water that's left in this jar to make matzo, the unleavened bread, for our poor seder. Still, you are welcome to share what little we have."

He nodded. "I will be grateful for that," he said. "I have not eaten these past two days." And indeed he looked very thin and hungry.

So the widow managed to scrape the barrel of the last grains of spelt, and, adding the few drops of water left in the jar, she made a batter for the matzo, baking it in the tiny wood-fired oven.

That evening Elijah, still in disguise, sat down to their small seder. The boy asked the Four Questions with ease. The mother served the matzo, though that was all the food they had. And Elijah told the story of the exodus from Egypt. Then he stayed the night in their barn.

The next morning he was gone.

The little boy asked his mother, "Where is the old man?"

"Gone on his travels," she told him. "He left me this note."

"Read it, Mama, please," the boy said, for though he had his alpha and bet, his letters, he did not yet know how to read words.

She began. "You gave me water when I was thirsty and fed me when I was hungry, though you had little enough yourselves. Do not despair, good woman. The Lord will help you and neither you nor your son will go hungry."

"Oh Mama, is it true?"

"It's only a wish from a sad old man," she said. "There is nothing more in the cupboard."

But the little boy went to the spelt barrel to see for himself. "Mama, Mama," he cried. "Look!"

When she looked, there was just enough spelt for another helping of matzo, and just the same amount of water in the jar that she'd had before giving half to the old man.

"Ah," she said, "charity comes back to the giver. Thank you, Elijah," for she realized who had been at her door. "And thank you, dear Lord."

Stories about the prophet Elijah *disguised as an old man, a dusty traveler, a stranger in town, are told and retold throughout all the Jewish communities.*

In all the stories, Elijah moves through time and around the world, bringing miracles to those who need it and to those who give charity— tzdekah—especially when they are impoverished themselves.

A version of this story, with a loaf of bread, not matzo, can be found in Azriel Eisenberg's Tzedakah: A Way of Life.

Matzo Balls

Matzo balls can be served in chicken soup or chicken broth. I like to make medium-sized matzo balls and serve two in each bowl, though I almost always go back for a third. This recipe, I believe, originally came from a can of matzo meal, but I have changed it over the years. Then I read online the hint about separating the eggs and beating the whites first, and that made them even better.

MAKES 15-20 MATZO BALLS

INGREDIENTS

4   eggs
¼   cup oil
¼   cup unflavored seltzer
1   cup matzo meal
1   tsp salt for the matzo mixture
1   tsp salt for the boiling water

EQUIPMENT

- 1 medium bowl
- 1 small bowl
- whisk
- electric mixer (optional)
- measuring cup
- measuring spoons
- rubber spatula or spoon for mixing
- large pot with a tight-fitting lid (a glass lid will help if you are not a patient cook)
- timer
- slotted spoon or tongs
- plate

1. Crack the eggs, and separate the whites from the yolks, dropping the whites into the larger of the two bowls and the yolks in the smaller bowl. Some chefs do this with their hands—holding the yolk in their hand and letting the whites pour down around through their fingers. You can also crack the eggshell in two and pour the yolk back and forth from one half shell to the other, letting the whites drip down into the bowl.

2. Whisk the whites until they are frothy. This will take some time and muscle. If you don't have these, you can use an electric mixer, but only for this step.

3. Using the hand whisk, add the egg yolks and mix gently but completely. (You do not want to whisk them the way you did the whites.)

4. Add in the oil and then the seltzer, mixing them gently into the eggs.

5. Add the matzo and salt, and mix them gently into the rest with a spatula or spoon.

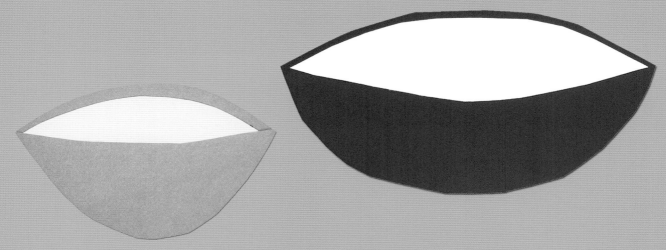

6. Cover, and refrigerate for at least an hour.

7. Bring a large pot of water and 1 teaspoon salt to a boil over high heat.

8. While the water is coming to a boil, wash your hands, but don't dry them. Take small amounts of the matzo mixture and make them into round balls. They will double in size while they cook, so make them half the size you want them. Set them aside on a plate.

9. Gently (so as not to splash yourself) drop each ball into the boiling water and, when they are all in (remember, they will grow to twice their size, so do this in two batches if your pot is not big enough), bring the water back up to a boil, then lower the heat to medium-low, and cover the pot with a lid.

10. This is the hard part: No peeking. Leave the lid on, and set a timer for 30 minutes. When it dings, turn off the heat, remove the pan from the burner, and reset the timer for 10 minutes.

11. After 10 minutes, uncover the pan, and remove the matzo balls from the water with a slotted spoon or tongs. When they have stopped dripping, put them on a plate. Serve them in soup, or refrigerate for the next day.

12. This recipe makes about 15-20 matzo balls, but don't worry if you have leftovers. Slice them up, and fry them in some butter or oil the next day.

MATZO IS A CRACKER-LIKE UNLEAVENED FLATBREAD. *It is made of plain flour and water.*

There are five grains that may not be used in any form during Passover, except for matzo: wheat, barley, spelt, rye, and oats.

Though matzo can be eaten as crackers all through the year, it is imperative to eat it in place of any breadstuff for the eight days of

Passover. This is done in memory of the unleavened bread the Jews took with them as they escaped from slavery in Egypt, as recorded in the Bible, in Exodus.

Some cooks use leaveners (like baking powder) in their matzo balls to keep them light and fluffy, but these cannot be served on Passover, when only unleavened food can be eaten.

❖ MAIN COURSES ❖

Rifka and the Magic Pitcher
Salad

The Pomergranate Seed
Pomergranate Couscous

How to Know a Noodle
Noodle Kugel

The Hair in the Milk
Matzo Lasagna

Three Clever Things
Tzimmes Chicken

Rifka and the Magic Pitcher

"For the Lord your God brings you into a good land ... a land of olive trees and honey."
—Torah, Deuteronomy 8:7–10

Long ago, a poor potter made a small living working from dawn to dusk. He worked hard and still got barely enough from his clay pots and pitchers to feed his growing family. There were six of them: his wife, his eldest daughter, Rifka, a pair of twin boys named Velvul and Aaron, and the youngest son, Shmuel, who was not yet walking.

Of all of them, it was Rifka who loved to watch her father work, for some day she hoped to be a potter, too. Not because she thought the work would be easy, but for how the clay felt under her fingers.

One day, when her father let her have a turn on the wheel, she made a pitcher. It was not as big as the ones her father sold at the market, but it just fit her small hands. She decorated it with olive branches and a slate-colored bird that sat with open eyes staring up at the handle.

Rifka was delighted with her creation, which she had made for her mother. "For milk," she thought. But when she looked inside the pitcher, to her surprise there were a few drops of something silvery at the bottom. She put her finger into the pitcher and brought it to her lips. To her surprise, it was olive oil. As she watched, the oil slowly rose in the pitcher until it was entirely full.

"Papa!" she cried, "come see." She held the pitcher out to him.
Now, he had watched her make the pitcher, and at no time had she taken it into the kitchen to pour in olive oil from the big barrel. He knew a miracle when he saw one. He said the word reverently.

"Oh Papa, can I take the pitcher to Grandmother? She has not had any olive oil to cook with or to light her lamps for weeks."

"My darling girl, you have a heart as big as the entire countryside. But I cannot let you go there alone. It is a long way."

But she begged and pleaded and promised to be careful, and because he loved her spirit, at last he let her go. He hitched their donkey to the cart, and added three other jugs—one filled with milk, one with honey, and one with vinegar, all for her grandmother. "Go slowly and carefully, my darling girl," he said, sending her off with a blessing.

Now, Rifka tried to be slow and careful, but the donkey had a mind of his own, and he went too fast over a bump. The big jugs had corks in them, but of course the little pitcher did not.

Bump! Thump! Some of the olive oil got shaken out of the pitcher.

Rifka was horrified. "Oh, what am I to do?"

Just then, a harsh-sounding voice from behind her in the wagon said:

> "Mizzle, fizzle, Rifka,
> Kick me in the kishka,
> Give me all your oil,
> And I will fly you there."

Well, Rifka knew immediately that the little voice was not really trying to help her. In fact whoever it was, he was trying to take advantage. So she said, "What good is it for me to take my pitcher to Grandmother's house if I arrive without the oil? I will do it on my own."

There was no answer, so on she drove. But again the little donkey sped up, and again *Bump! Thump!* went the cart. And some more of the olive oil got shaken out of the pitcher.

And again came the little voice behind her.

> "Mizzle, fizzle, Rifka,
> Kick me in the kishka,
> Give me all your oil,
> And I will fly you there."

This time Rifka turned around, put her hands on her hips, and said, "I see no one there behind me. I shall get to Grandmother's on my own."

A little further down the road and *Bump! Thump!* went the cart for a third time. And some more of the olive oil got shaken out.

> "Mizzle, fizzle, Rifka,
> Kick me in the kishka,
> Give me all your oil,
> And I will fly you there."

By this time—because three is a mystical number—Rifka had figured it out. She stopped the little donkey, then turned entirely around and said, "You are a wicked imp. You are the cause of all these bumps and thumps and spills." She also guessed that the imp had to be somewhere in one of the corked jugs. So she scrambled into the back of the cart and started to pull out the corks.

One, she pulled out the cork from the milk jar. *Thwwwwwp!* But no one was there.

Two, she pulled out the cork from the honey jar. *Thwwwwwp!* But no one was there.

Three, she pulled out the cork from the vinegar jar. *Thwwwwwp!* With a *piff, pop, poof,* Rifka, donkey, cart, and all were sitting in front of her grandmother's house.

She laughed and clapped her hands. There, sitting on the ground, legs crossed, and looking furious was a hideous little man no bigger than her father's knee.

"Are you that wicked imp?" she asked.

> "Imp I may be, and not so fine,
> But all that oil should have been mine!"

He stamped his foot once, twice, and on the third stamp he vanished.

Just then Grandmother came out of the door, and when she saw Rifka, she held out her arms. Rifka raced into them, and they laughed and laughed.

"Come see what I've brought you," Rifka said.

Together they took down the corked jugs one at a time and brought them into the house. But when Rifka returned for the little pitcher of oil, she discovered that there was nothing left in it. She began to weep and picked it up to take it into the house. But the minute she picked it up, the oil began to fill again, higher and higher until the pitcher was completely full.

Grandmother had come out of the house and saw what had happened. She knew, as well as Rifka's father had known, that this was a miracle. "Tell me all about it, child."

When Rifka finished telling the story, Grandmother said, "I understand now. If you had given that imp what he wanted, the pitcher would have lost its miraculous power. But now it will remain full as long as you hold it in your hands."

Using the magical pitcher, Rifka was able to fill every available jug at Grandmother's house with the oil, which they then took to the market to sell. Grandmother never had to worry about doing without oil—or anything else—again. And as for the potter and his family, they were rich enough to share with all their neighbors till the end of their days.

For a slightly different telling, *see* The Diamond Tree: Jewish Tales from Around the World, *by Howard Schwartz and Barbara Rush.*

If you think this story sounds a bit like "Little Red Riding Hood" in parts, you are correct. It also has echoes of the imp in "Rumplestiltskin."

The original story was collected from Jews who lived in Iraq. It certainly illustrates how important olive oil has been in the Middle East.

Salad

In my family, it's not dinner unless something green is served. Or as my niece and nephew say, something "growing." This simple, colorful salad smells as good as it looks and tastes. Add or subtract any "growing" ingredients you like, or make the salad just the way the recipe is written.

MAKES 6 SERVINGS

INGREDIENTS

1   large or 4 Roma tomatoes

1   large or 2 small cucumbers

½   red, yellow, or orange pepper

4   scallions (green onions)

1   garlic clove

1½   tbsp olive oil

     juice of half a lemon

2   tbsp fresh parsley

1   tbsp fresh mint

     salt and pepper to taste

EQUIPMENT

• cutting board

• knife (serrated works best for tomatoes)

• peeler

• spoon

• large bowl

• small bowl

• measuring cup

• large spoon

• scissors (optional)

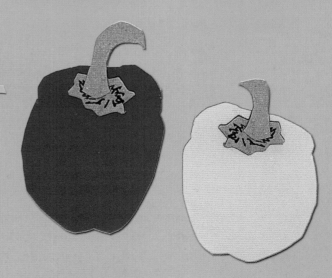

1. Rinse the tomatoes, onions, herbs, and the lemon.

2. Tomatoes: Cut in half lengthwise, and with clean hands, scoop out the seeds with your fingers. Chop the meaty tomato parts into bite-sized pieces.

3. Cucumbers: Peel the dark green skin, and cut in half lengthwise. With a spoon, scrape out the seeds, and chop the remaining cucumber into pieces the same size as the tomatoes.

4. Pepper: Cut in half and remove all the seeds and the white insides. Chop half into small pieces.

5. Scallions: Chop off the top and bottom ends. Peel off the first outside layer, and chop scallions into small pieces.

6. Garlic: Peel the papery outer layer and mince (chop into tiny pieces).

7. Herbs: Cut with scissors or chop into ¼-inch pieces.

8. Lemon: Squeeze into a small bowl and, if necessary, pick out the seeds.

9. Toss all the fruit (tomatoes are a fruit) and vegetables in a large bowl.

10. Sprinkle the olive oil over the salad, and toss. Repeat with the lemon juice.

11. Add the chopped herbs and a pinch of salt and pepper. Toss and taste. Add more salt and pepper if needed.

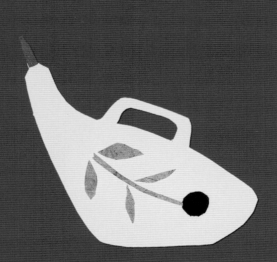

OLIVE OIL IS MADE BY PRESSING THE FRUIT OF THE OLIVE TREE *(Olea europaea).*
It was not only used for cooking, but also served as fuel for oil lamps.

The first pressing yields "extra virgin" olive oil. "Extra light" refers to the color, not the calorie count of the olive oil.

Wild olive trees have been written about for at least 2,200 years. The earliest documents speak of olive oil being used in religious rites in ancient Minoa (part of Greece). By the Iron Age (eighth to sixth centuries BCE), people cultivated olive trees on stepped terraces.

Olive oil was also used for soap, cosmetics, money, and was poured daily into the seven cups of the golden menorah at the Holy Temple in Jerusalem. It was also used for anointing priests and kings.

Cloudy olive oil or solid pieces floating in it doesn't mean it has gone bad. It has been cold and only needs to be brought back up to room temperature.

The Pomegranate Seed

"May it be Your will, O Lord our God, that our good deeds will increase like the seeds of the pomegranate."
—Rosh Hashanah prayer

A hungry Jew, whose family was starving, stole a loaf of bread from the market. But as soon as he slipped the loaf into the waistband of his trousers, the stall owner began to shriek, "Thief! Thief!"

The man began to run, but he was no better at running than he was at stealing. Within three or four steps he felt the heavy hands of the sultan's guards on his shoulder.

They marched him off to prison, where in the near dark of his cell he found a single pomegranate seed on the dirt floor.

"Why is the Lord plaguing me?" he thought. "Here I am about to be executed for stealing a loaf of bread so that my children would not starve, and He sends me a pomegranate seed."

But, since the rabbis always said, "The Lord does not toy with us," he gave that seed much thought.

When the guards brought him out to the open courtyard for his execution, the Jew was ready. He turned his face up to the executioner and spoke so loudly, everyone—including the sultan, himself—could hear, "Kill me as you must, but do not throw away my magic pomegranate seed."

"What nonsense is this?" growled the executioner.

"Not nonsense at all. If you plant it, it will grow instantly into a great pomegranate tree, laden with ripe fruit. But ..." the Jew shrugged.

"But what?" The executioner lowered his axe and leaned forward.

"The seed will only grow if you have never stolen anything. So you see, it is useless to me now."

The executioner trembled. "I have taken things from the pockets of those I have executed, instead of giving it to their heirs. I cannot plant the seed."

The Jew held up the seed to the guards. "Is there one among you who can plant the seed?"

The guards conferred amongst themselves. Finally, one came forward. "We have each taken golden spoons from the sultan's table. We cannot plant the seed."

The thief turned to the sultan's vizier. "And you, mighty sir?"

The vizier trembled. "I have ... um ... occasionally pocketed coins from the sultan's treasury. Ummmm ... coins owed to me." He looked quickly down at the ground.

"Then, magnificent sultan, it is up to you to plant the seed," the Jew said.

The sultan smiled. "And haven't I taken entire countries from other sultans? I doubt I could plant that seed."

"Oh mighty and powerful people, you have taken trinkets, coins, golden spoons, entire countries, and still retain your high status and wealth. And here am I, a poor Jew, who only wanted to feed his starving children. Yet you will live and I will die."

The sultan laughed. "What a clever man you are. I need someone like you around to remind me how a life can be saved by a simple pomegranate seed." He made the Jew a royal gardener and moved his family into the palace, where they never went hungry again.

⁘

WE FOUND FOUR VERSIONS OF THIS STORY: *in Peninnah Schram's* The Hungry Clothes and Other Jewish Folktales, *as "The Pomegranate Seed"; in Sheldon Oberman's* Solomon and the Ant and Other Jewish Stories, *as "The Magic Seed"; in Nathan Ausubel's* A Treasury of Jewish Folklore, *as "The Wise Rogue"; and in Barbara Diamond Goldin's* A Child's Book of Midrash, *as "The Clever Thief."*

This story is originally from Morocco, but stories about Jews (and Arabs) who manage by cleverness to get themselves out of impossible situations are quite popular throughout the Middle East.

In some tellings, the thief is Jewish, in others he is not. But the story is a popular one amongst Middle Eastern Jews.

This is Tale Type 929—"Clever Defenses" and K 500—"Escape from Arrest by Trickery."

• •

Pomegranate Couscous

You can serve couscous in hundreds of ways, starting with plain and getting as fancy as you like. As kids, my brothers and I refused to eat couscous, which we called "sea sand," because of its texture. So when I make it, I add all sorts of goodies. If the ones in this recipe aren't available (where I live, pomegranates are only sold around the winter holidays), find something else that looks delicious in your pantry or at the store. I like the colors in this dish, and honestly, if you put fresh cilantro and mint on just about anything, I will eat it.

I make this dish with both Israeli couscous, which is a pearl-shaped creamier couscous, and Moroccan-style couscous, which has finer grains. When you choose the type of couscous, make sure to note the differences in the ratio of water to couscous, as well as the different cooking times in the recipe. But whichever you choose, they are both delicious.

MAKES 8 SERVINGS

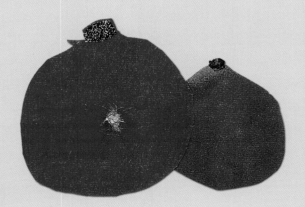

INGREDIENTS

2   tbsp pine nuts

1   small onion (or ½ large onion)

2   tbsp margarine or butter

10 dried apricots

½   tsp salt

    pinch of cinnamon

1   tbsp chopped fresh cilantro

1   tbsp chopped fresh mint

    handful of pomegranate seeds

Israeli (Pearl) Couscous:

1   cup uncooked couscous

2   cups water (or any 2 to 1 measurement)

Moroccan Couscous:

1   cup uncooked couscous

1   cup water (or equal parts water and couscous)

EQUIPMENT

- medium-sized skillet
- plate
- knife
- cutting board
- spatula
- measuring cup
- measuring spoons
- scissors (optional)
- medium pot, with lid
- bowl of water for separating the pomegranate seeds

1. On the stove, heat a skillet to medium, and toast the pine nuts. Shake the pan gently while they cook so they don't burn. After about 3 minutes, turn them out onto a plate to cool.

2. Chop off the ends of the onion, peel away the outer layer, and chop it into small pieces.

3. Chop the apricots into small pieces.

4. Melt the margarine (or butter) in a skillet at medium heat, and then add the onion. Cook until the onion pieces look sort of see-through (approximately 5 minutes), stirring often.

5. Lower the heat, add the apricots, salt, and cinnamon, and heat through (about a minute). Remove from the heat and set aside.

6. Measure and pour the water into the pot and bring to a boil.

7. Add the couscous and cook:
—Moroccan: Remove from heat and let sit 10-12 minutes.
—Israeli (pearl): Cover and let boil at low heat about 10 minutes until all the water is absorbed. Stir occasionally.

8. Rinse and chop the cilantro and mint. Hint: The best tool for this is a pair of clean scissors.

9. Fluff the couscous, and add the onion-apricot mixture, pine nuts, herbs, and pomegranate seeds. See note below about pomegranate seeds.

Deseeding a Pomegranate: Be careful, because pomegranate juice stains. Fill a bowl with water in the sink. On a cutting board, cut the top off the pomegranate—it's the side with the stem sticking out. Then carefully cut into the skin in about six places, from the open end all the way to the bottom (think of it like the earth—from the North Pole all the way to the south, in a straight line). But only through the skin, don't cut all the way into the fruit. Put the pomegranate in the bowl of water. With your hands, separate the seeds from the white pulp and skin. The seeds will sink and the rest will float. Throw out the floating bits and what you have left are the seeds. Drain, and use.

THE POMEGRANATE'S LATIN NAME IS PUNICA GRANATUM; *the "punica" refers to the Phoenicians, who were so important to the cultivation of the fruit.*

Pomegranate means "seeded apple."

In the Bible, the pomegranate (rimmôn) is spoken of as one of the seven fruits that Israel was blessed with. In Jewish tradition the pomegranate is a symbol of righteousness, because its 613 seeds (or arils) supposedly correspond to the 613 mitzvoth, or commandments of the Torah. This is one of the main reasons Jews eat pomegranates on Rosh Hashanah, though the number of seeds actually varies with the individual fruit.

VARIATIONS: *This recipe is flexible. To make more or less, simply adjust the dried couscous and water measurements.*

Pomegranate seeds are seasonal. If you can't find them, try substituting dried cranberries. I have actually found pomegranate-infused dried cranberries, which are yummy. Put them into the pan with the apricots. Don't like pine nuts? Leave them out, or try some other kind of nut instead. The sweetness of this dish is from the apricots. Leave them out for a completely different flavor.

The pomegranate tree was originally native to regions from Iran to the Himalayas, though over the centuries it has been brought into the Mediterranean and Eastern Africa, and was even introduced into Latin America and California by Spanish settlers.

Traditional couscous has to be steamed several times to come out light and fluffy. But, in modern grocery stores, it is possible to buy instant couscous that makes the cooking both easier and quicker.

Couscous is different from pasta because it is toasted—traditionally on an open flame.

How to Know a Noodle

"You say it's pudding, I say it's kugel!"
—Aunt Vera Krassner to the author

Hershel Ostropolier was a wit and a wag; he saw the humor in any situation and always used it to his advantage. And what could be funnier than for Hershel Ostropolier to go into a top restaurant in Minsk, Pinsk, or Vilna without any money. He would eat and eat and then complain that the food was bad or that he'd found a roach in the cream cake or a rat in the milk. He would groan and tell the owner that the cake or the milk was no longer kosher. And then he would refuse to pay.

Funny—if you were Hershel Ostropolier.

Not so funny if you owned the restaurant.

Now, one day, Hershel went into the fanciest restaurant in Minsk and ordered kugel made with egg noodles. He ate most of it but left enough on the plate to make his point.

When it was time for the bill, he turned to the waiter and said—in the tone of a rich man used to being obeyed—"Bring the manager at once."

When the manager arrived, looking frizzled and frazzled, Hershel said, "I cannot believe that you call that mess a kugel. A kugel should be made with egg noodles. Sweet or savory. With vegetables. Or meat. Or fruit. But always noodles first. You call that noodles? I do not think so."

"I beg your pardon, sir," said the manager, "but they *are* noodles."

"Do you even know what noodles are?" Hershel said in a withering tone.

The manager called over the waiter. "Get me the chef."

Soon enough the chef came out, and Hershel said to him, "Do you even know what noodles are?"

The chef said to the waiter, "Get me the potboy."

Hershel smiled to himself. He knew he was about to win. If they had to call the potboy, Hershel would get out of paying once again.

Out came the potboy in a worn apron that was covered with stains, a yarmulke on his head. His hair was pulled back, and he had the beginnings of a beard.

"Our potboy is studying to be a rabbi and he is used to answering questions. Surely he can answer yours," said the chef. "He spends his days trying to define things and his evenings working here at the restaurant."

Hershel asked the potboy, "So, do you even know what noodles are?"

The potboy scratched his head and looked at the bit of kugel left on the plate. He pointed to the noodles. "Good sir," he said to Hershel, "*those* are noodles."

Hershel laughed. "And why should we call those stringy, slimy, inedible things noodles?"

The potboy said, "Why, sir, they are long like noodles. They are soft like noodles." He picked up one and slurped it down. "They taste like noodles. So why shouldn't they be called noodles?"

For the first time in many years, Hershel Ostropolier was not able to make a witty reply. And for the first time in many years, Hershel Ostropolier had to pay for his dinner.

Hershel Ostropolier is a popular Jewish trickster character. He has been called a Jewish Till Eulenspiegel. Many stories are told about his pranks. In half of them he gets away with everything (including murder), and in others he gets his just rewards.

One of the Yiddish books in which Hershel stars is Ruth Levitan's A Sheyner Gelekhter. We found a variant of this story in Nathan Ausubel's A Treasury of Jewish Folklore, which is in English.

There is debate about whether Hershel Ostropolier was a real person or a fictional character. Some scholars say he was born in the Ukraine in the second half of the eighteenth century, living between 1750 and the early 1800s. According to these sources, he became a kind of court jester to Rabbi Boruch of Miedzyborz, the hereditary tzaddik, or holy man, who suffered from melancholy. It was Hershel Ostropolier's job to make the rabbi happy—a tough job.

Even if Hershel Ostropolier was real, his legend has expanded over the years, and it is difficult to say which stories come from the real life and which from the fictional scamp.

Some famous Jewish writers who wrote or retold stories about Hershel Ostropolier include Sholem Aleichem and Eric Kimmel.

Don't try to tell my family that kugel isn't supposed to be sweet and custardy. No matter how many times I try to make this side dish in other ways (like my great-aunt Rose's crispier version with raisins), my kids only like this sweet recipe. If you want a bigger kugel for a holiday dinner, double the recipe. You may have leftovers, but I have never known kugel to go to waste, since it tastes good the next day, either cold or reheated.

MAKES 6 SERVINGS

INGREDIENTS

6–8 ounces of uncooked egg noodles

2 eggs

2 tbsp butter (soft)

2 tbsp milk

½ tsp vanilla

½ cup ricotta cheese (or cottage or pot cheese)

2 oz cream cheese

¼ cup sour cream

¼ cup sugar

¼ tsp cinnamon

butter to grease the pan

EQUIPMENT

• large pot

• strainer

• large bowl

• electric mixer or whisk

• measuring cup

• measuring spoons

• large spoon

• 2-quart casserole or glass baking dish

1. Fill a large pot ¾ full with water, and bring to a boil. Cook the noodles according to the package directions (usually about 5–7 minutes), drain them, and set aside.

2. Preheat oven to 350°F.

3. Crack the eggs in a large bowl, and beat them with an electric mixer or whisk.

4. Add the butter, milk, vanilla, ricotta cheese, cream cheese, sour cream, sugar, and cinnamon.

5. Mix well with mixer or large spoon.

6. Add the cooked noodles, and stir with a large spoon.

7. Grease the bottom and sides of a 2-quart baking dish, and pour (or spoon) the noodle mixture into the pan.

8. Bake, uncovered, for 30 to 40 minutes, or until the tips of the noodles sticking up the most get golden brown and the custardy middle has set.

VARIATIONS: *Add golden raisins to the noodle mixture before cooking.*

For a sweet crunchy topping, crush about ½ cup of corn flakes, mix in 1 teaspoon of sugar and ½ teaspoon of cinnamon, then sprinkle the mixture over the top of the kugel before baking.

KUGEL IS PRONOUNCED EITHER COO-GAL OR KEY-GILL, *which is how it is said in Galicia.*

Kugel is a noodle side dish or pudding that can have many added elements: vegetables, fruit, or even meat, if the family does not keep kosher.

The kugel became a staple in Jewish cooking because of the limitations on doing any work on the Sabbath. The dish could be made before the Sabbath eve and kept in a slow-cooking warm oven whose fire had been kindled before the Sabbath, as well.

Kugel originated in Germany, where the Jews made their own version of the German gugelhupf, a ring-shaped cake. The Jewish version added eggs, cottage cheese, and milk or cream. Later, in the seventeenth

century, sugar was added, and kugel then became a dessert when made with fruits, as well as a main dish when made with vegetables.

The first published American recipe for kugel was in 1871 in Esther Levy's Jewish Cookery Book.

Some Hassidic Jews (ultra orthodox) believe that eating kugel on the Sabbath brings with it special mystical powers. When a certain Hassidic rabbi eats with his followers, and the kugel is brought out, they believe that at that very moment "the rabbi has the power to bestow health and food, and even to help couples conceive," according to Allan Nadler, a professor of religious studies at Drew University.

Kugels today range from blueberry or sour cherry or rhubarb to potato or broccoli. There is even a three-layer kugel with sweet potato, broccoli, and cauliflower.

The Hair in the Milk

"No human hand touches these matzos."
—B. Manischewitz Co. slogan, 1880s

A woman named Nadia was close to giving birth and sent for the old midwife, Tante Reisha. Now Tante Reisha was old, but she knew more than all the other midwives in the community, for her mother and grandmother before her had been midwives as well.

Soon after Tante Reisha arrived at the house, one of the servants brought Nadia a glass of milk. Nadia took the glass and was about to drink it when she turned as white as the milk, and fainted.

While the servants fanned Nadia and put cold compresses on her temples, old Tante Reisha picked up the glass and stared into it. A long black hair floated on the top of the milk. Well Nadia was blonde, and her servants all had light-brown hair, so Tante Reisha shook her head and said, "Tsk-tsk-tsk!"

Quickly she poured the milk back into the jug, corked it tightly, and, with both hands, shook the jug until whatever was inside began to scream. Then Tante Reisha put her ear to the side of the jug and listened until she heard a voice call from inside, "Let me go. I beg you. Let me go."

Telling the servants, "I am taking this cursed jug outside to deal with it; lock all the doors and windows behind me," Tante Reisha went out and waited until one of the servants waved at her from a window to say that all had been done. Then the midwife slowly pulled out the cork and peered into the jug.

Pop! The head of a beautiful woman came out of the jug, her long, lustrous black hair trailing behind her.

Tante Reisha knew at once who it was and immediately put the cork back in the bottle, catching the woman by her hair. But magically the jug was now too heavy for her to lift. For the first time, she was terribly afraid and made the sign against the evil one with her right hand.

"Lilith," she cried, "be gone." For she knew the black-haired woman was the demon Lilith, Adam's first wife.

Lilith's voice was soft and cozening. "Set me free, old woman, and I will do you no harm."

Tante Reisha was not afraid for herself. Lilith harmed only newborns, and sometimes their mothers. But Nadia and the child in her womb were in Tante Reisha's care, so she had to find a way to vanquish the demon.

"First," said Tante Reisha, "tell me how to revive the mother."

Lilith laughed. "Why should I do that? The mother and child are mine!"

Tante Reisha felt cold at the bone. With one hand, she grabbed Lilith by her long hair, with the other hand she uncorked the jug. She knew that a demoness is helpless when held by the hair.

"Let me go, let me go," Lilith begged weakly.

But Tante Reisha held on. "Not until you tell me how I may save this woman and child from you once and for all."

Lilith was defeated … for the moment. She answered truthfully, because she had to. "Take saliva from her mouth and put it in a bucket of water."

Still holding tight to Lilith's hair, Tante Reisha explained this loudly through the locked window to a servant. Quickly this was done, and the servant brought the bucket outside.

Lilith bent over and blew the foam on the top of the water, as if skimming it, and Nadia awoke from her faint. This the servants reported through the locked and bolted windows.

"But tell me, demoness, how did you manage to get in the house in the first place?" Tante Reisha asked. There were *mezuzot* on every door, with the word of the Lord written on sacred paper inside each one.

Lilith laughed again, but it was a sad laugh, for Tante Reisha had still not let go of her hair. "The mezuzot were defective, and the family did not think to have an amulet against me hung over the infant's bed." She sighed. "*Now* will you set me free?"

But Tante Reisha did not let go of the demoness' hair. "There is more you must promise. Or I will cork you back into the milk bottle, put it in a great chest, and fling it into the sea." She turned Lilith toward the water that was just steps away from Nadia's house.

The demoness shuddered, for she could hear that Tante Reisha meant every word. "What do you want?"

"That you will serve this family in every way and protect mother and child from danger for three years—danger from yourself and any other demons who would try and hurt them." Tante Reisha knew that after three years, the child would be safe from the demons who only hunted newborns.

"And if I do not agree?"

Tante Reisha did not speak directly to Lilith, but turned instead to the servant who had brought out the pail. "Bring me one of your mistress' clothing chests."

The servant ran back into the house, locking the door behind.

Then Lilith understood she had been beaten. The midwife knew all the tricks. That was the trouble with old women. They know everything. "Very well," she said, "I vow I will do as you say. No other demons will go against my wishes, for I am their queen."

Tante Reisha knew this was true. But she remembered the last thing her mother and grandmother had taught her. "Then swear it in the names of the angels Senoy, Sansenoy, and Semangelof," for those were the three angels who had taken control of Lilith when she'd run from Adam.

Lilith so swore. She had no choice.

For three years, the queen of the demons remained at Nadia's house, doing chores as a servant would do—cutting wood, pumping water, making bread, lighting fires. And most importantly, she kept Nadia and her little girl, Rachael, safe from harm.

As for Tante Reisha, she had the house mezuzot repaired and came to Nadia when her other children were born. She brought with her amulets to put over their little beds to keep them safe from demons. And never again—though she always checked—did Tante Reisha find Lilith in another milk jug.

THIS STORY, ORIGINALLY FROM THE TURKISH KURDISH TRADITION, *can be found in a slightly different telling in Howard Schwartz's collection,* Lilith's Cave, *which he found in the Hebrew book* Shishim Sippurei Am, *edited by Zalman Baharav.*

According to Midrash stories and folklore, Lilith was Adam's first wife. When she was denied equality, she ran from Eden, which prompted Adam to complain to the Lord, who sent three angels to bring her back. Found living with demons, Lilith was warned that one hundred of her demon children would die daily if she didn't return. She refused and was punished. Her revenge was to kill as many human infants as she could and, sometimes, the new mothers.

Jewish parents believed they could ward off Lilith by putting an amulet with the names of the three angels around the newborn's neck or hanging the amulet above the cradle. You can still see these amulets in some communities.

The mezuzah *(*mezuzot, *in the plural) is sometimes called the "Jewish lightning rod." It is a small rectangular case affixed to each doorpost in a house. Inside are two verses from Torah, handwritten on parchment in tiny Hebrew script. The first is the* Shema, *known as the watchword of the Jewish faith—"Hear, O Israel: the Lord our G-d, the Lord is one." All who pass that doorpost touch the* mezuzah *and kiss the hand that touches it, remembering the verses and what they mean.*

Matzo Lasagna

Lasagna is an Italian dish, so what is it doing in this book? My daughter's friend Jonah once said to me, "Heidi, do you know what it's like to celebrate a birthday during Passover, when you can't eat cake?" This got me thinking. What do you do when you can't eat your favorite foods? The answer—make them anyway! If you can't eat pasta for Passover, make the dish with something *else*. Voilà—matzo lasagna. This dish is delicious and fun to make, too. We love it with spinach and mushrooms, but it is perfect without either. My girls also like it with eggplant, which I sauté in olive oil before adding it into the layers.

MAKES 6 SERVINGS

INGREDIENTS

16   oz container of cottage cheese

1   egg

2   cups shredded mozzarella cheese

½   cup grated Parmesan or Romano cheese

14   oz jar of spaghetti sauce

3   full sheets of matzo

4   large mushrooms (8 oz)

     handful of baby spinach leaves

EQUIPMENT

- bowl
- spoon
- measuring cup
- cutting board and knife (if the mushrooms are not sliced already)
- 8 x 8-inch baking pan
- aluminum foil
- spatula for serving

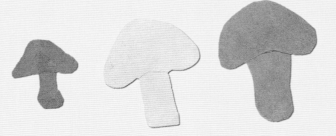

1. Mix the cottage cheese, egg, and half the mozzarella and Parmesan (or Romano) in a bowl.

2. Wash and slice the mushrooms, and rinse and dry the spinach leaves.

3. Preheat the oven to 350°F.

4. Spoon a small amount—just enough to cover the bottom—of spaghetti sauce into the bottom of an 8 x 8-inch pan.

5. Lay a full sheet of matzo on top of the sauce, and then spoon more sauce on top. Spread it out with the back of the spoon.

6. Spoon half the cottage cheese mixture onto the sauced matzo, and spread it out. Top with another matzo and sauce.

7. Lay the handful of spinach leaves on top. Smooth them out, and spoon sauce on top, spreading it out.

8. Spread on the rest of the cottage cheese, and top with sliced mushrooms in a single layer.

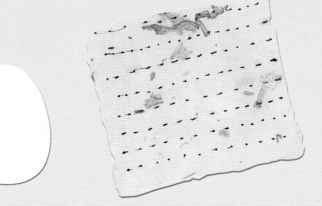

9. Spread more sauce on top, and then another matzo topped with sauce.

10. Finally, top with the remaining mozzarella, and sprinkle on the remaining Parmesan (or Romano).

11. Cover with foil, and bake in the oven for 40 minutes.

12. Remove the foil, and bake for 10 more minutes.

13. Let the matzo lasagna sit for at least 10 or 15 minutes before you serve it.

VARIATIONS: *Matzo lasagna is perfect plain (without the spinach and mushrooms). If you make it this way, you can add an extra layer by only using ⅓ of the cottage cheese in each layer and adding an additional sheet of matzo, topped with sauce, in the middle. If you like your lasagna saucier, add more sauce to the layers—it will be a bit more bubbly and a bit soupy. Or, if you are feeling ambitious, find a recipe for homemade sauce.*

THE WORD LASAGNA REFERS NOT ONLY TO THE ITALIAN DISH, *but also the noodles themselves. Though not a traditional dish, matzo lasagna is one of many creative dishes for a new world of Jewish cooking. Substitutions (like the matzo for noodles) mean you can cook greater varieties of food during the holidays.*

Though some people are opposed to food not steeped in tradition (or passed down through the generations), most modern Jews welcome these new meals to their holiday tables and all year long.

Since this is a milk dish, it can become the main course in a milk meal for a family that keeps kosher. The word kosher *originally meant "good" or "proper," but now simply means an item "fit for ritual use." Certain*

animals, for example, cannot be eaten because they are not considered kosher: pig, camel, rabbit, crab, lobster, octopus, and swordfish, among others.

The tradition of not serving meat and milk dishes at the same meal derives from a line in the Torah that speaks of "not boiling a kid in its mother's milk" (Exodus and Deuteronomy). At a meat meal, one cannot also have milk, cream, or cheeses of any kind, not for three to six hours afterward. Cheeseburgers? Forbidden. Mozzarella cheese sprinkled on spaghetti with meat sauce? A no-no. In fact, many ultra orthodox households have two separate sets of cooking/serving utensils, dishes, silverware, potholders, and sometimes even two refrigerators, two stoves, and two dishwashers—one for meat and one for milk.

Three Clever Things

"Roast chickens don't fly into your mouth."
—OLD JEWISH SAYING

"Don't make a tzimmes out of it!"
—YIDDISH/ENGLISH SAYING MEANING *"DON'T MAKE A BIG DEAL"* OUT OF SOMETHING.

A man named Mr. Abrams moved from Jerusalem and bought a fine house in the provinces. Soon everybody knew who he was, for he was generous and kind.

Mr. Abrams wanted to invite his son Solomon, who still lived in Jerusalem, to come see the house and land. But before he could write the letter, he fell very ill and knew he was about to die. So he called in his housekeeper, Benjamin, and gave him a package. In that package was a letter telling his son how much his father loved him and blessed him. The package also contained a list of all his worldly goods, and they were many.

"Promise me," Abrams said to Benjamin, "that if someone claiming to be my son Solomon comes from Jerusalem, give this package to him as his inheritance—but only if he is truly my son. If he can do three clever things for you, he is the one. Otherwise tell him I have died and left him nothing. For if the young man is *not* clever, then he is *not* my son after all."

Though he was weak, Abrams further arranged with Benjamin to warn everyone in town not to disclose his address to any stranger who inquired. "If it is Solomon," he said, "he will figure out how to find me."

Thus saying, Mr. Abrams shut his eyes and died.

Not long after, Solomon arrived. Though all he knew was the name of the town, he was sure he could find the place his father was staying. But ask as he might, he could get no one to talk to him.

Finally, he saw an old man carrying a load of twigs, his back bent double with the effort.

Solomon went over to him. "Good grandfather," he said, "will you sell that load of twigs to me?"

Of course the man was more than willing.

"And for an extra sum will you deliver it to Mr. Abrams, who is newly come to your fair city?"

The old man took the money and carried the twigs to the house, his pledge not to tell any stranger of Abrams' whereabouts intact.

Wordlessly, Solomon followed him.

The twig man called out to Benjamin, "Come and take this load of twigs!"

Benjamin looked out the open window and exclaimed, "I bought no twigs from you."

The old man said, "True, you did not. The load belongs to this young man following me."

Benjamin looked where the twig man pointed and immediately recognized Solomon, who was very like his father. "That's one clever thing," Benjamin whispered under his breath.

He opened the door wide. "Come in, come in," he said to Solomon, and when they were seated and having a cup of sweet tea, he asked Solomon why he was in the town.

Solomon looked over the rim of the teacup. "I am the son of the man who owns your house. Will you take me to him?"

"Alas," Benjamin said, "your father died last week. In the morning I will show you his grave. There are many rooms in this house, and one shall be yours for as long as you wish."

"My father—gone? But I didn't have time to say goodbye." Solomon wept silently.

Benjamin's wife, Mina, came in at the door and heard this. "He died in peace and with no sins on his head. He left you his love and blessings."

"That is all I wished for," said Solomon.

"Then come and have dinner with our family," said Benjamin, "for Mina is here to bring us in to eat."

Mina had indeed prepared a fine dinner. When the men joined Mina and the family at the table--the two sons and two daughters were already there—Mina brought out a platter with five roasted chickens. She set this before Solomon.

As soon as evening prayers over the food were said, Benjamin told their guest, "If you are truly your father's son, you will serve us equally. Your father did so often enough, and now it is your turn."

Of course this was a test, for there was no way to divide five chickens evenly between seven people.

Solomon shook his head. "This is not mine that I should serve it."

Benjamin looked at him and smiled. "But I *truly* wish you to."

So Solomon knew it was another test that his father had probably posed for him. He took a moment to look at the five chickens and then at the six people, plus himself. Using a long fork, he set one chicken on a plate between Benjamin and his wife, a second between the two sons, a third between the two daughters, and the final two on his own plate.

The family ate without making any comment. But when they were done, Benjamin said, "Explain to me how you divided the chicken, for it seemed to me that you took more than your share and left us with less."

Solomon grinned. "You, your wife, and one chicken total three. Your two sons and one chicken total three. Your two daughters and one chicken total three. And I, with two chickens, total three. So how have I taken any of your portion?"

"Papa! Papa!" cried the children, "how clever his answer is."

Two clever things, thought Benjamin.

The next evening, after Solomon had worked in the fields all day with his host, they sat down to dinner again. This time Mina brought in a single fat roasted chicken and once again asked Solomon to serve.

Once again, Solomon shook his head. "This is not mine to share out."

Once again Benjamin said, "But I *truly* wish you to."

Solomon looked carefully at the roasted chicken, and then at the family. Carefully he carved the meat, giving the head to the host, the entrails to the wife, the two thighs to the sons, the two wings to the daughters, and set the whole body of the chicken on his own plate.

The family ate without making any comment. But when they were done, Benjamin said, "Explain to me how you divided the chicken, for it seems to me that you took more than your share and left us with less."

Solomon smiled. "I gave the head to you, Benjamin, because you are the head of the house. I gave the entrails to your wife,

Mina, because children issued from her womb. The two thighs went to your sons because they are the pillars of the house; the two wings to your daughters because soon they will fly away from your house to their husbands. I took the body, which is shaped like a boat, because I came in a boat and will leave in one."

"Papa! Papa!" cried the children, "how clever his answer is."

Three clever things, thought Benjamin. *Just as Mr. Abrams said.*

"Now come and give me my father's letter," said Solomon, "for I am sure he told you to try me with three tests. Surely I have passed."

"You are as wise and clever as your namesake," said Benjamin, "but not clever enough to realize that this house and all that is in it belongs to you. That, too, your father left you, along with his love."

"Then I leave it for you and your family who dealt ethically with my father and with me," said Solomon. "I have no need of a house here. All I want is my father's blessing." "And you have ours, too, kind son of a kind father," said Benjamin as he gave his guest the letter that Mr. Abrams had left in his keeping.

···

THIS STORY WAS SENT TO ME BY MAGGID JIM BRULE, *from Fayetteville, New York, a friend of a friend who collects Jewish stories.*

The tale is from Midrash Rabbah—Lamentations 1.4. Midrash is a particular rabbinical way of reading and explaining, or understanding, scripture. The rabbis' stories and explanations can be found in books of Midrashim (the plural of Midrash). Sometimes, as the rabbis wrestled with alternative readings of the Torah, folkloric stories became part of the Midrashim.

Midrash stories will most often have a moral core. In this one, Solomon is both clever and wise. But he also practices tzdekah, Jewish charity, for in the end, he gives the house and land to the people who cared for his father.

· ·

Tzimmes Chicken

Though my mom loves tzimmes, my kids never did. Until, that is, I started cooking the dish with a roasted chicken. My version is a bit more subtle than the traditional bold flavors of tzimmes, and I usually substitute pearl onions (a favorite in my house) for the prunes. But remember, all cooking is about experimenting, and substitutions are always welcome, either because you don't have an ingredient, or because you don't like it.

NOTE: When working with chicken, or any raw meat, it is important to wash your hands with soap and water after almost every step and then again at the end. You should also wash all the surfaces you have touched.

FEEDS A FAMILY

INGREDIENTS

1	whole chicken
1	sweet potato
4	carrots
4	apples
10	prunes
1½	tsp salt
1½	tsp pepper
1	orange
½	cup apple cider
2	tbsp honey
2	tbsp brown sugar
¼	tsp cinnamon
¼	tsp nutmeg
¼	tsp allspice
¼	tsp ginger

EQUIPMENT

- peeler
- knife
- cutting board
- large bowl
- small bowl
- measuring spoons
- measuring cup
- zesting tool (optional)
- juicer (optional)
- large spoon or spatula
- large roasting pan
- paper towels
- aluminum foil

1. Peel the sweet potato, and cut it into small- to medium-sized pieces. Peel the carrots, and cut into coin-like pieces. Wash 3 of the apples, and cut (leave the skin on but remove the core and seeds) into 6 to 8 pieces each. Put all these into a large bowl with the prunes.

2. Mix the salt and pepper in a small bowl.

3. Wash the orange, and cut it in half. Squeeze the juice of one half, and if you have a zesting tool, zest that half. Zesting means removing the orange part of the skin in very small shavings.

4. In a measuring cup (or a small bowl), mix together the apple cider, honey, orange juice and zest, brown sugar, cinnamon, nutmeg, allspice, ginger, and a pinch of the salt and pepper mix.

5. Pour the sauce over the vegetables and fruit, and toss. Set aside.

6. Preheat the oven to 425°F.

7. Remove the chicken from its wrapping, and remove anything from the cavity (usually there is a bag of giblets inside. You can throw these out unless you wish to use them in another recipe later.) Rinse the chicken in cool water, and put it (breast-side up) in the center of a roasting pan.

8. Pat the chicken dry with paper towels, and pour half the salt and pepper mixture into the cavity of the chicken.

9. Wash your hands.

10. Fill the space around the chicken with the fruits and vegetables, and pour any sauce that is still in the bowl over them, but not over the chicken.

11. Cut up the remaining apple (removing the core) and the un-juiced orange half. Stuff those into the cavity of the chicken.

12. Sprinkle the remaining salt and pepper mixture onto the skin of the chicken.

13. Tent the chicken with a piece of aluminum foil: cut a piece of foil and lay it loosely across the top. You want to cover the bird with the foil, but leave it open— you are protecting the skin from burning, but you do not want the chicken to be steamed by the juices in the pan.

14. Bake for 1 hour, then remove the foil and cook for 15–20 more minutes to crisp up the skin. If you have a meat thermometer, stick it in the chicken (try not to touch bones); it should read at least 165°F.

15. When you remove the chicken, let it sit for about 15 minutes before carving.

TZIMMES (ALSO SPELLED TSIMMES) *is an Eastern European/Russian Jewish recipe that can be either a side dish or a main dish.*

Tzimmes is made of diced or sliced carrots, yams, or squash, combined with onions and dried fruits like raisins, prunes, apricots, pineapples, or apples. The flavorings are traditionally honey and cinnamon, and sometimes a bit of ginger. This is a slow-cooking casserole meal, over low heat.

There are several explanations for the name. One is that it comes from German, combining the words zum *(for) and* essen *(eating). Another is*

VARIATIONS: *This recipe is two recipes combined, and each can be easily changed to suit your tastes. In our house, we like our tzimmes with onions. I add half a bag of frozen pearl onions to the carrots. Try dried apricots in addition to (or instead of) the prunes. Use squash. Experiment with the spices, too. Tzimmes traditionally has warm, sweet flavors, but this chicken can be seasoned and stuffed with lemons and thyme or oregano, instead of apples and oranges, and surrounded by potatoes and carrots instead of tzimmes.*

that it comes from Yiddish through Middle High German and means "a light meal." A third is that the word tsimmes *comes from the word* simmer, *which, of course, means "slow cooking," even though it is baked.*

A favorite Sabbath meal, tzimmes is also served on Rosh Hashanah and Succoth. On Rosh Hashanah, carrots are traditionally used because the Yiddish word for carrots is meren, *which also means "to increase." In other words, tzimmes is a wish that one's fortunes and good deeds should increase in the new year.*

❖ DESSERT ❖

The Pastry That Was Eternally Dirty
Rugalach

The Congregation That Loved Jam
Hamantaschen

Two Jars of Honey
Honey Cake

The Little Cap-Wearers and the Cow
Mini Cheesecakes

The Pastry That Was Eternally Dirty

"One even gets tired of eating rugalach."
—JEWISH SAYING

There was once a very rich man named Pinchas who was also a terrible miser. He hated spending money on anything. His wife and children lived as if they had no money at all, because the miser simply wouldn't give them a copper coin.

Now, one day Pinchas was walking along the street. He had just bought a small piece of pastry, rugalach I think it was, at the poorest stall in the market. Not paying attention, daydreaming as usual about new ways to save money, he dropped the rugalach on the ground. Looking around to be sure no one saw, he picked it up, dusted it off, and kept walking.

Now along came a beggar. Let's call him Shmednik. He saw Pinchas and, though he didn't know him for a rich man, he knew the man had bought something at the market, which made him rich in Shmednik's eyes. "Please, sir," Shmednik said, "may I have a coin to get something to eat?"

"Here!" said Pinchas, handing the beggar the dirty pastry. And, thinking that he'd solved two problems at once, he headed happily home.

Now that night in his thin bed, Pinchas dreamed that he was in the city, sitting at a large, crowded café. The waiters were running about like mad men, bringing each customer piles of delicious tortes and cakes and pastries, and especially rugalach. The smell was delicious. The taste was delicious. In his dream, Pinchas smacked his lips.

But no matter how many of the customers had their plates piled high, not a single pastry found its way to Pinchas's plate.

Pinchas waited and fumed. He fumed and waited. At last he began to complain. "What am I?" he said loudly, "Chopped liver?"

No one answered.

"I can pay. Do you think I cannot pay?"

Still no waiter came to his table.

Finally Pinchas stood. He shouted, "I want something to eat!"

A waiter came to him and handed him a piece of dirty rugalach.

Pinchas's jaw dropped. His eyes squinted. His hand shook. "Is this some kind of joke? How dare you bring me this filthy pastry. Did I ask for charity? I am a rich man. I can pay!"

The waiter bowed his head. "I am sorry, sir, your money cannot buy anything here." His hand made a circle that took in all of the café.

"I don't understand," Pinchas said.

"You have just arrived in Eternity," the waiter said. "This is where you come after you die. And all you can eat here is what you sent on from your life before, what you gave in charity to those with less than you. Evidently, all you sent ahead was this one dirty piece of pastry, so that is all I can give you." He dropped the thing on Pinchas's plate, and left.

A STRAIGHTFORWARD VERSION OF THIS STORY *may be found in* Jewish Folktales, *retold by Pinhas Sadeh. No one is named in the story, and it is pretty bare-boned. Another version, called "Cake," is in Josepha Sherman's* Rachel the Clever and Other Jewish Folktales. *Both Sadeh and Sherman use an oral tale from Tunisia as the base story.*

In Judaism, charity (tzdekah) is always emphasized. From the earliest days of the Jewish people, sharing with the poor, the needy, the unfortunate has been an important part of what makes a Jew. For example, there are even rules about how to let the poor glean (pick up leavings in a harvested field), stating they may do it three times a day!

In Jewish stories, the miserly always end up in trouble, while those who give away everything they own are the ones who get back all they have donated to the poor—and more.

Parallel stories to "The Pastry That Was Eternally Dirty" have been found in Eastern Europe and Egypt. Cakes, tarts—and even cookies—are the pastries in those stories.

Rugalach

This is the perfect cookie dough—simple to make, and how can you go wrong with butter and cream cheese? I find that the best tool for making rugalach is a pizza cutter.

MAKES 48 COOKIES

INGREDIENTS

Dough:

1   cup butter (2 sticks)

8   oz cream cheese

2   tbsp sugar

   pinch of salt

2   cups all-purpose flour

   extra flour for rolling out the dough

Filling:

1   cup walnuts (ground)

¼   cup brown sugar (packed)

1   tsp cinnamon

¾   cup jam (apricot or currant)

Topping:

1   egg

1   tbsp milk

   cinnamon sugar

EQUIPMENT

- measuring cup
- measuring spoons
- large bowl
- electric mixer or large spoon
- wire colander or sifter
- plastic wrap
- food processor
- medium bowl
- large surface (countertop or board)
- rolling pin
- butter knife
- pizza cutter or knife
- small bowl
- fork
- spoon or brush
- cookie sheet
- spatula

1. Let the butter and cream cheese soften to room temperature.

2. With an electric mixer or large spoon, mix the butter, cream cheese, sugar, and salt.

3. Sift the flour into the dough bit by bit, mixing in each batch.

4. Wash and dry your hands, then rub some flour between them to prevent sticking.

5. Using your hands, make sure all the ingredients in the dough are well mixed, and separate the dough into round dough balls.

6. Wrap the dough balls in plastic wrap, and refrigerate for an hour.

7. While the dough is chilling, grind a handful of walnuts in a food processor, and measure 1 cup. Mix the ground nuts with the brown sugar, cinnamon, and jam. Set aside.

8. When you are ready to roll out the dough, preheat oven to 350°F.

9. Sprinkle flour onto a clean surface and rub around with clean hands. Rub flour on a rolling pin. Remove the plastic wrap from the dough.

10. With the rolling pin, roll out the first dough ball until it looks like a flat pizza—lifting it off the floured surface and flipping it over several times while rolling, adding more flour if necessary.

11. With a butter knife, spread some of the nut and jam mixture onto the dough.

12. Using a rotary pizza cutter or a knife, cut the dough like a pizza, straight down the middle, and then again, perpendicular to the first cut. Continue making pizza slice–like cuts until you have made 16 pieces.

13. Roll up each piece of dough starting with the curved edge (if it were a pizza slice, you would be starting with the crust).

14. Lightly beat the egg and milk in a small bowl with a fork. With the back of a spoon or a brush (I actually prefer to use my fingers), brush the top of the uncooked cookie with the egg wash.

15. Sprinkle with cinnamon sugar.

16. Place on a cookie sheet, and bake in a 350°F oven for 25 minutes.

17. Remove with a spatula to cool before serving.

VARIATIONS: *You can cut the dough into triangles instead of making big balls and*

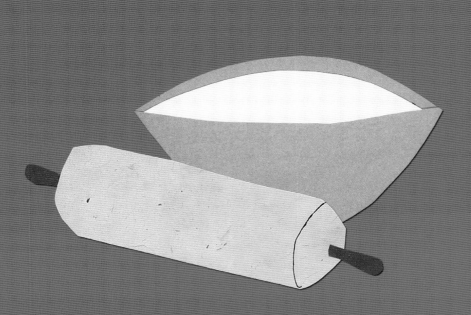

slicing them like pizza. You can also use different types of nuts and jams in the filling. Experiment to find which ones you like best. Try using a different type of filling in each batch.

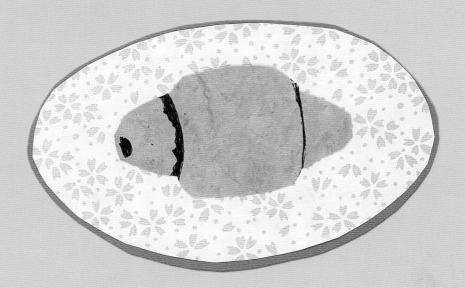

LIKE OTHER SWEET PASTRIES, *rugalach are very popular at Rosh Hashanah, the New Year, because of the wish that the coming year be a sweet one. But rugalach can be served at any event or party.*

Is it spelled rugalach or rugelach or rugaleh? The spelling seems to change arbitrarily. So take your pick.

Rugalach are easily frozen and keep for months in the freezer.

The Congregation That Loved Jam

"We'll nosh on hamantasch-en."
—CHILDREN'S PURIM SONG

Rabbi Moshe was much beloved by his congregation, even though he often played tricks on them. But the tricks always contained a lesson.

On this particular Sabbath, right before the reading of the Torah, the rabbi went up to the reader's table. He leaned forward, and spoke quietly, so quietly everyone in the congregation had to lean forward to hear what he had to say.

"My dear friends," Rabbi Moshe said, "if there are those among you who love jam, you are invited to my house after the service."

A buzz rose up from all the people, for who doesn't love jam?

Now, as soon as the service was done, the rabbi went right back home. He ate his lunch, then lay down for a nap. Had he forgotten the invitation? Not at all, but a little rest after eating was his Sabbath routine.

Had his congregation forgotten the invitation? Not at all. They gathered in the rabbi's courtyard, waiting for his door to open. But the door stayed closed, and no one knew what to do.

A minute passed, then fifteen, then a half hour, finally an entire hour, and still the door remained shut.

"Should we knock?" Motl the Tailor asked.

"Best not," cautioned Hyman the Butcher.

"He might be resting," said Simcha the Schnorrer, who, himself spent a lot of time resting.

"He's probably praying," said Malka the Matchmaker.

And on and on they gabbled until another hour had passed.

But, jam, the rabbi had said. They would wait.

Suddenly at three o'clock, by Simon the Baker's pocket watch, the rabbi's front door opened, and there he was.

"Are you all here?" asked the rabbi.

"All here," they answered, eager to sample the jam.

"Good, good," said Rabbi Moshe, "and in that case, you can all now turn around and go home."

"Go home?" they asked. Surely they had not heard him right.

"Yes," the rabbi told them, "for now I know how many of you truly love jam." He closed the door. They could hear him laughing on the other side.

And home they went, shrugging. Nobody was angry. The rabbi had played another trick on them. A trick with a lesson. His usual kind.

And the lesson? Listen with your ears, not your stomach.

THIS YIDDISH STORY, *in a shorter, pared-down version, can be found in* Yiddish Folktales, *collected by Beatrice Silverman Weinreich and translated by Leonard Wolf. It was originally found by the longtime collector Khaim Sheskin in the town of Grodno, in Poland.*

Rabbis are not usually the jokesters in Jewish folklore, but this story is both about a joke and the rabbi teaching his congregants an important lesson about greed.

Hamantaschen

MAKES 35

INGREDIENTS

Dough:

¾   cup (1½ sticks) butter, room temperature

½   cup sugar

1   egg

2   tbsp milk

1   tsp vanilla

1   tsp baking powder

2¼   cups all-purpose flour

     extra flour for rolling out the dough

Filling:

Choose a filling: jam, fruit preserves, chocolate (Nutella or chocolate chips), apple butter, halvah spread, poppy seed filling or try a combination.

EQUIPMENT

- measuring cup
- measuring spoons
- large bowl
- electric mixer or large spoon
- wire colander or sifter
- plastic wrap
- large surface (countertop or board)
- rolling pin
- round cookie cutter or a drinking glass with a round opening
- small bowl
- fork
- kitchen brush
- cookie sheet
- spatula

1. With an electric mixer or a large spoon, cream together the butter and sugar.

2. Add the egg, milk, vanilla, and baking powder, and mix.

3. Sift the flour into the mixture a bit at a time, mixing with a spoon or electric mixer until it gets too tough, then use your (clean) hands to finish the job.

4. Wrap the dough in plastic wrap, and put it in the refrigerator for an hour or overnight (so it is cold enough to roll out). You can break the dough into 3 or 4 balls and wrap them individually, or wrap the entire ball.

5. When you are ready to roll out the dough, preheat the oven to 350°F.

6. Remove the dough from the refrigerator and flour your hands, a clean surface, and the rolling pin.

7. Separate the dough into workable portions if you have not already done so. With a rolling pin, roll out the dough with plenty of flour so it doesn't stick. It should be about ¼-inch thick.

8. Cut the dough into circles using a round cookie cutter or the opening of a drinking glass. Set aside.

9. When the circles are cut out, scoop a dollop of filling onto each cookie right in the middle. Fold up the sides—making 3 folds to create a triangle—and pinch the dough-corners of the triangle together. There should be filling still showing in the center.

10. For a golden-brown color, beat one egg with a tablespoon of milk or water, and brush the cookies before they go into the oven. (If you like your hamantaschen doughier you can skip this step.)

11. Bake for 20 minutes or until the top has browned a bit.

12. Remove with a spatula to cool before serving.

VARIATIONS: *Though jam is the easiest, you can make all sorts of hamantaschen fillings. Try using prepared pie fillings or making your own poppy seed filling.*

HAMANTASCH IS THE SINGULAR AND HAMANTASCHEN, *the plural, but nowadays hamantaschen may be used for both. Some linguists believe the cookies were originally called* mon-taschen, *which is Yiddish for "poppy seed pockets."*

Hamantasch is a three-cornered cookie eaten during the Jewish holiday of Purim. Purim celebrates the triumph of the Persian Jews over an evil vizier who planned to have them all destroyed.

There are two explanations for why the cookie is three-cornered. One is that it represents the three-cornered hat of the villain Haman,

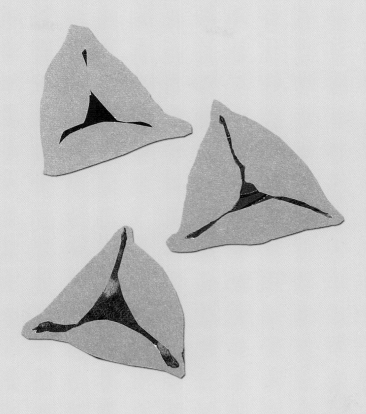

who wanted to hang all the Jews. However, because of the king's brave and beautiful Jewish wife, Esther, it was Haman himself who was hanged. The second story is that they represent Haman's big ears. And in fact, in Israel hamantaschen are called Oznei Haman, which means "Haman's ears."

Traditional hamantaschen fillings are poppy seeds, chopped or pureed prunes, dates, or apples, or any numbers of different jams, including apricot, strawberry, raspberry, even orange marmalade. The tradition of filling the cookies with poppy seeds came from Central Europe, and plum or prune fillings came from the area that is now the Czech Republic.

Two Jars of Honey

"If you deal in honey, there's always a chance for a lick."
—Jewish saying

Once, in the time of King Solomon, a beautiful widow named Shifre was courted by the lord of the city. The lord of the city was a bad man, miserly and mean. He had his servants beaten for small mistakes, and his wives—he'd had five of them—beaten as well.

Fearing that if she stayed, she would be forced into a marriage with that wicked man, Shifre ran off to her parents' home, many miles from there, with only the clothes on her back. Everything else—her house, her bedding, her cooking pots—she left behind.

But before she went, she had put all the silver and gold in the house into two large jars, which she filled to the brim with honey. Then she took those jars to her neighbor, Miriamne, saying, "I am off to my parents'. I pray you, keep these honey jars for me until I return."

Miriamne agreed, put the honey jars on a shelf in the barn, and promptly forgot about them.

· · · ·

Well, time passed, and more time, and Shifre did not return. Just as she had forgotten the jars of honey, Miriamne all but forgot her old neighbor as well.

Time passed some more, and Miriamne's son Aaron was about to celebrate his bar mitzvah. She began to bake honey cakes for the celebration, but as she baked long into the night, she ran out of honey.

Exhausted from all the work for the party, Miriamne began to weep. "I shall spoil Aaron's bar mitzvah, and he will never have another." It was then that she suddenly remembered the jars of honey that Shifre had left all those years earlier.

"I shall use those jars," Miriamne thought, "and after the bar mitzvah, I will buy new honey for the jars. If Shifre returns, I will tell her that we used the contents for Aaron's cakes and then refilled the jars."

Of course, when she had used up all the honey, Miriamne found the gold and silver hidden at the bottom—coins and bracelets, necklaces and belts, and even a small crown. Absolutely thrilled at her newfound wealth, and forgetting that it did not belong to her, she danced around the kitchen, all exhaustion forgotten.

Quickly she rinsed each precious item carefully, then wrapped them in cloth, and hid them under her bed. She told no one but her husband. And he considered the new wealth theirs as well.

As soon as the bar mitzvah was over, Miriamne's husband bought honey, and they refilled the two jars, setting them back in the barn.

· · · ·

Well, time passed, and more time, and the wicked old lord of the city died, friendless and unmourned. When Shifre heard this, she said a fond farewell to her parents and went back to her house in the city. After cleaning the place from top to bottom—for you can imagine how dusty it had gotten after all that time—she went over to Miriamne's to ask for her two jars of honey back.

Miriamne and her husband handed her the jars, and closed their door quickly after her. Not noticing how strangely her neighbors acted, Shifre took the jars home, spooned the honey into other pots, and, to her shock and horror, discovered that all her treasures were missing.

She ran into the street crying, and knocked on Miriamne's door. Guessing who was knocking, Miriamne didn't open it.

Poor Shifre, everything she had was gone—coins and jewelry, and even the small crown she had worn at her wedding to her beloved husband. What would she live on? How could she go on?

She went to the judge of the city and then to the Sanhedrin court, and was told by each that without a paper signed by the neighbors when she gave them the jars, or a witness willing to testify that she had put the treasures in the honey, they could not take her case.

Shifre came back to her house, sank down on the doorstop, and began to weep.

Just then, Solomon, a boy and not yet a king, passed by on his way to the yeshiva. He was young—but already wise beyond his years. Stopping in front of the sobbing woman, he said, "Dear Auntie, why do you weep?"

She looked up and wiped her eyes. "Child, it is a puzzle that the judge and the Sanhedrin court cannot rule on, so I shall not trouble you with it."

Solomon shook his head. "Do not judge me by my age. My father is King David, and I will plead your case to him. Come." He nodded at Shifre, and she arose and went with him to the great palace.

When Solomon came in with the still-beautiful old woman, King David was seated on his great throne.

"Father," Solomon said, "this woman has been wronged, and I would judge her case."

David laughed. "You are much too young, my son. You should be at your studies."

"Life is the greatest study of all," Solomon countered. "Let me try this case, and you can watch."

So David gave Solomon his crown and let him sit on the throne.

Then Solomon said to Shifre, "I will send two guards to the house of your neighbors. They are to bring back Miriamne and her husband, and the two jars of honey."

Quickly it was done as Solomon said. And soon before him stood Shifre and her neighbors. The guards set the two jars of honey by the throne.

First Solomon turned to Shifre. "Do you swear that when you gave these two jars to your neighbors, there was a treasure hidden at the bottom?"

"I do," Shifre said, her voice low and throbbing.

"And that when you received them back, the jars contained nothing but honey?"

Shifre nodded. "Nothing but honey."

Then the boy Solomon turned to Miriamne and her husband. His face was stern, but it was still a boy's face, and Miriamne's husband smiled slyly.

"And do you swear," Solomon said, "that the jars held nothing but honey when you received them, nothing but honey all the while you kept them, and nothing but honey when you gave them back?"

"I do so swear," said Miriamne, trembling just a little.

"She does so swear," added her husband, triumphantly.

"Then," said Solomon, his boy's voice rising so that all in the room could hear him, but especially the guards, "smash the jars."

The guards seized the honey jars and smashed them, first one and then the other. At the bottom of the second jar was a single gold coin, sticking to the honey.

"Ah," said King David.

"Ah," echoed the guards.

Miriamne flung herself at Solomon's small feet. "I will return all," she said. "They are carefully wrapped and hidden beneath my bed. I just needed the honey for the honey cakes for my son's bar mitzvah party."

Solomon told the guards to go again to the neighbors' house and find the treasures under the bed. They did so quickly and gave everything back to Shifre.

Shifre turned to Miriamne and gestured to the two honey jars. "The honey I give you freely," she said. "I do not begrudge you that. Let us forget the rest and call it a mistake."

Matching Shifre's compassion, first Solomon and then King David dismissed the case and put neither Miriamne nor her husband in jail. Miriamne made more honey cakes and delivered half to her neighbor, who brought them to young Solomon.

"For your first judgment," she told him, "and the sweetest one you shall ever make."

I FOUND FOUR VERSIONS OF THIS STORY. *In Peninnah Schram's version, the judgment is rendered by the local wise woman. In both Josepha Sherman's and Ellen Frankel's versions, the judgment is by the young David, but in Pinhas Sadeh's collection it is attributed to the young Solomon. We chose to give this version to Solomon as he is the king most noted for his wisdom, even as a child.*

King Solomon (in Hebrew: Shlomo) was the son of King David and his wife Bathsheba. According to the Bible, he "excelled all the kings of the earth in riches and in wisdom." He was born in the tenth century and ruled Israel for about forty years.

There were no names of characters in the versions by Frankel and Sadeh, but it seemed to make for a smoother telling to name the two women.

In Biblical times, foodstuffs like honey were stored in large earthenware jars.

Bar mitzvah is the ceremony in which a boy of thirteen "becomes a man." (The bat mitzvah for girls at 12 is a much more recent ceremony.) Held on a day near the child's birthday, the ceremony includes the boy (or girl) reading from the Torah in Hebrew and speaking about the text to the congregation. The Torah is the scroll containing the Five Books of Moses (known by non-Jews as the Old Testament). Afterward, the bar mitzvah boy (or girl) is considered an adult ready to follow Jewish law.

Honey Cake

I like my honey cake dense and rich, while my daughters like theirs light and fluffy. So in my house, we compromise with this recipe. No matter how you like it, though, the one thing honey cake should never be is dry. Honey cake is traditionally made with coffee, but since no one in my house drinks coffee, it is not an ingredient I have on hand in my kitchen. One day, when we wanted honey cake, I found a bottle of cola someone left in my pantry (none of us drink soda, either) and decided to substitute it for the coffee. It tasted great! So now I keep a bottle of soda in the back of my pantry just for honey cake.

INGREDIENTS

2	eggs, separated
½	cup packed brown sugar
2	tbsp oil (vegetable, corn, canola—any light cooking oil)
2	tbsp applesauce
¾	cup honey
½	cup cola
1¾	cup flour
1	tsp baking powder
1	tsp baking soda
1	tsp cinnamon
¼	tsp ground cloves
¼	tsp nutmeg
¼	tsp ginger

EQUIPMENT

- 2 medium bowls
- electric mixer or whisk
- measuring cup
- measuring spoons
- sifter or wire colander
- rubber spatula or large mixing spoon
- loaf pan
- parchment paper (optional)

1. Preheat the oven to 325°F.

2. Crack the eggs, and separate them into the two bowls.

3. With an electric mixer or a whisk, beat the egg whites until they are frothy.

4. Add half the brown sugar (this is not a precise measurement, just use about half) and beat into the egg whites. Set aside.

5. In the second bowl beat the egg yolks, then add the rest of the brown sugar, as well as the oil and applesauce. Mix.

6. Add the honey and cola to the egg yolk mixture, and mix. If you are using the electric mixer, be careful—the batter is very thin and may splatter.

7. Sift the flour and other dry ingredients through a wire colander or sifter into the yolk and honey mixture, adding it bit by bit, mixing with a rubber spatula or mixing spoon, until everything is incorporated.

8. Add the egg white mixture, and fold in gently by hand (so as not to lose the fluffiness), until it is all mixed.

9. Tear off a piece of parchment paper big enough to line the loaf pan, and press it into the pan, folding where needed, and laying it against the sides as flatly as possible. There will be extra parchment paper sticking out—this is fine. (If you don't have parchment paper, you can use baking spray or butter and flour to grease the bottom of the pan.)

10. Pour in the batter, and bake for 70 minutes or until a toothpick inserted into the middle of the loaf comes out clean.

11. Remove by pulling the edges of the parchment paper that are sticking out. Peel the parchment paper off and set the loaf to cool. You can eat it hot, or wrap it for the next day.

VARIATIONS: *Some recipes for honey cake include nuts and raisins. Or if you like a more traditional cake, use brewed coffee instead of the cola.*

HONEY HAS BEEN PART OF THE HUMAN DIET FOR AT LEAST **10,000** YEARS. *There is a Mesolithic rock painting found in a cave in Valencia, Spain, showing two honey hunters taking honeycomb from a wild bee's nest.*

Honey cakes are traditionally served on Rosh Hashanah, the Jewish New Year, or for other special occasions. "May the New Year be sweet," as the wish goes.

The honey cake is also a symbol of the land of Israel, the "Land of Milk and Honey" (Exodus 33:3).

In some Jewish congregations, on Rosh Hashanah small straws of honey are given out to everyone who comes to temple. It is also traditional at

Rosh Hashanah to eat apples dipped in honey, so some honey cakes are made with apple juice.

Some cooks make their honey cakes two to three days ahead, storing them for the holidays, because the flavor gets better and moister over time.

Honey cakes are not just Jewish treats. They are also popular in Britain, Europe, Greece, India, and in Russia, as well as the former USSR states, where they are often served up as Lenten cakes.

There are literally hundreds of varieties of honey, made from hundreds of kinds of flowers. Honey made from wildflowers is called polyfloral. Honey made from one specific flower source is called monofloral. Honey made by mixing together several kinds of honey is called blended. Some flower blossoms that are used for honey you could probably guess: clover, orange, apple, sage, lavender, alfalfa, avocado, blueberry, strawberry, thyme, almond, aster, blackberry. And some may surprise you, like cactus, catnip, cotton, black locust, eucalyptus, grapefruit, mesquite, and ivy.

The Little Cap-Wearers and the Cow

"Go to a land flowing with milk and honey."
—Torah, Exodus 3:8

There was once a dairyman named Tevye who had four milk cows that all went dry on the very same morning.

"Trouble always comes in threes," Tevye told his wife, "but this is four. Four cows, four dry. I smell something fishy, and it isn't carp." He realized that someone must be stealing into his barn and milking the cows until they were dry.

"A thief is a thief," he added, "whether it is milk or money. I will have to think up a plan to catch that *goniff*."

That night, Tevye brought a chair and a blanket into the barn. Lighting the lantern, but dimly, he set it down near the cows and sat in the darkest corner to watch. Just past midnight, he heard footsteps. He knew it was not his wife, for she slept like the dead, except that she snored.

Into the barn crept a tiny man and woman, so small they fit comfortably *under* the cows. They both wore extraordinary caps—the man's hat had a large floppy brim, the woman's tied about with ribbons, a ribbon under her chin holding it in place. They settled themselves on tiny stools, set buckets beneath the cows' udders, and began to milk.

Oy! were they fast milkers, the fastest Tevye had ever seen. They'd finished one cow and were on to the next in the blink of an eye.

Tevye leaped up, shouting, "Stop! Stop, you little cap-wearing thieves! Stop!" He threw off the blanket as he ran toward them. The little man was too fast and was off in a flash, but Tevye caught the little woman by the ribbons on her hat, holding her high in the air. "I should beat you!" he shouted, though he wouldn't have done any such thing.

The little woman began to cry. "Spare my life, and I promise we'll never come back. And your cows will give you twice as much milk as ever before."

Tevye didn't know if he should believe her, but what else could he do? So he let her go, having given her such a fright.

But all that the little woman said came true. She and her man never returned, and those four cows gave as much milk as eight for the rest of Tevye's life, and beyond.

A SLIGHTLY DIFFERENT VERSION OF THIS STORY *can be found in* Yiddish Folktales, *part of the* Pantheon Fairy Tale and Folklore Library, *where it is called "Who's Milking the Cows?"*

The story is also slightly reminiscent of Grimm's fairy tale #39, the "The Shoemaker and the Elves," though in this case the elfin folk are not helping the milkman/shoemaker, but rather, stealing from him.

This dairyman is named Tevye after the most famous Jewish dairyman— Tevye in Sholem Aleichem's wonderful stories, which were eventually made into the brilliant musical Fiddler on the Roof.

The dairyman was a familiar sight in Eastern European Jewish villages. In fact nearly half the Jews in those towns owned at least one cow or goat for their own household use. But if they needed more milk than the one cow could provide, both the rich and the poor would buy their milk from the local dairyman. With any leftover milk, the dairyman would make cheese.

Mini Cheesecakes

Cheesecake may not be a traditionally Jewish dessert, but it is most certainly served at many family gatherings and holidays. These mini treats are fun to make and are my own twist on the no-bake cheesecake.

MAKES 24

INGREDIENTS

Crust:

8-9 chocolate Graham crackers
    (1 cup crumbs)

2 tbsp butter

1 egg

Cheese mixture:

⅓ cup heavy cream

8 oz cream cheese

½ cup sugar

1 lemon

Garnish:

blueberries, strawberries, raspberries, blackberries (choose one or use a variety)

EQUIPMENT

- food processor or zip-sealed bag
- small pan or microwave-safe bowl
- measuring cup
- cookie sheet
- spatula
- 2 bowls (3 if you are not using a food processor)
- electric mixer or whisk
- knife
- mixing spoon or rubber spatula
- spoon for scooping

1. Preheat the oven to 350°F.

2. Grind up the graham crackers to a fine powder in a food processor or seal them in a bag and crunch them with your fist.

3. Melt 2 tbsp butter either on the stovetop at medium-low heat or in the microwave for about 30 seconds in a microwave-safe bowl.

4. Mix the egg and the butter into the graham cracker crumbs (using the food processor, if you are using one) to make the crust dough.

5. Pull off a small piece of the dough, and roll it into a small ball in the palm of your hands. Press the ball partly flat (about ¼-inch thick), and set it onto a cookie sheet. This is the base of your bite-sized cheesecakes, so the size is up to you. Add more melted butter if necessary.

6. Make another and another until you are done. They should look like brown coins.

7. Bake for 7 minutes, and remove with a spatula right away. Let cool completely.

8. In one bowl, using a whisk or an electric mixer, whip the cream just until it is stiff. Set aside.

9. Squeeze the juice from the lemon into the second bowl, and pick out any seeds.

10. Add to the lemon juice 8 ounces cream cheese and the sugar. Mix using an electric mixer or spoon.

11. By hand (with a spoon or rubber spatula, not an electric mixer), mix the whipped cream into the cream cheese mixture. Refrigerate for an hour or more.

12. When the cream cheese mixture is fully cold, plop a spoonful onto each chocolate coin and top with a berry.

13. Refrigerate until serving time. These cakes can be made up to a day before you plan to serve them.

VARIATIONS: *Try using a pastry piping bag to pipe the cream cheese mixture onto the crust. Sprinkle cocoa power, colored sugar, or sprinkles onto the top. Experiment with different toppings instead of fruit—a chocolate chip or a fresh mint leaf are delicious, but use your imagination.*

For an extra fancy dessert, serve with paper doilies under each mini cheesecake.

THIS IS A FAVORITE RECIPE FOR SHAVUOT, *the Jewish festival that celebrates the giving of the Torah to Moses at Mount Sinai, as well as being a harvest festival. As such, Shavuot is one of three Jewish festivals that link history and harvest, the other two being Passover and Purim.*

Dairy foods are traditional for Shavuot because reading the Torah is said to be "milk and honey under the tongue."

The first historical mention of cheesecake is during the 776 BCE Olympics, when it was served to the athletes.

Cheesecake is made with all sorts of dairy products, including, but certainly not limited to, cream cheese, buttermilk, sour cream, farmer's cheese, cottage cheese, and ricotta.

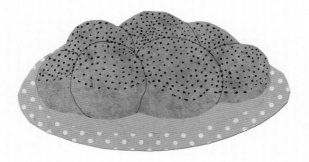